Teaching Music Theory

Teaching
Music Theory

by

KARL ESCHMAN

James King Wiltsee Professor of Music
Denison University

E. C. SCHIRMER MUSIC COMPANY
600 Washington Street   Boston, Mass.

MT
6
.E 84

By the same author:
CHANGING FORMS IN MODERN MUSIC

E.C.S. No. 1812

Teaching Music Theory

Preface

This is not, I hope, a pretentious book. It does not strive to be original since the fundamental materials in this field are common property. What I write is based upon personal experience and presents the convictions and, I trust, the insights of a teacher.

What this means may be illustrated by the imaginary response of two musicians in the same situation: let us assume that a student is having difficulty in recognizing the sound of a certain melodic interval. The first musician will soon say, "If you cannot go directly from the sound to the recognition by name you do not belong in music; choose some other field." Not so, the true teacher; he will be con-

Preface

stantly seeking ways to help the student's recognition and to "save" the student through progressive understanding for a field in which he may already have some dexterity as a performer. This book will suggest devices that have proved useful in this and many other situations.

I shall not hesitate to speak in simple terms or to use the language of an elementary classroom in the illustrations. Some of the methods presented differ from the formal statements of texts on harmony. The approach is an integrated one containing much more than the traditional content and suggesting far-reaching application in advanced courses. Harmony is fundamentally the ordering of the musical vocabulary in syntax and conjunction. While the words or chords in vertical structure of this vocabulary may increase almost without limit, certain fundamental principles govern the tonal language and these we need to present to our students in the clearest and most efficient manner. This book deals primarily with tonal harmony because of the belief that students should master that field before they consider a style of writing based upon the duodecuple or 12-note scale of so-called atonal music. A thorough understanding of harmonic procedures is also basic to mastery and fluency in the writing of contrapuntal textures, again within tonality. Bruckner, Hindemith and Schönberg

Preface

insisted upon such a foundation, according to all reports of their teaching. To borrow an analogy from the visual arts, we would like to think that a painter is able to draw something that looks like a human face before he starts to throw paint at the canvas from a distance. Similarly we believe a musician in the present day needs a strong technical foundation. We must not waste his time; this foundation should be secured in the most efficient and practical way, and while it is being secured, his creativity must be nurtured and encouraged. It is with this purpose in mind that the book has been written.

I am indebted to James Haar as editor for his meticulous assistance in the preparation of the manuscript. My special thanks go to my friend George Sherman Dickinson, who read this text in its earlier version and offered encouragement as well as many suggestions. However, he is not to be considered responsible for methods or opinions presented here. I was determined to avoid much of the detail which an exhaustive discussion of every possibility in each situation would have added, and to present only the important essentials. Teaching is nothing if not personal or individual and therefore, in the sense that each person is a unique individual, original as well. Although far from conventional language of theory at times, the book's statements may, I

Preface

hope, be suggestive. All our discussions in this non-material art of music must be based upon similes and parallels of a rather crude sort. If we could not use these inexact, yet suggestive symbols we would have to keep silent or communicate only in musical sounds.

This book is addressed to teachers of musical theory and to those advanced students who are ready for generalizations in theory; however, the methods suggested will have application at many different levels, from primary through secondary to college education. The better the preparation of the prospective teacher in advanced theory, the better the teaching at the most elementary level may become. I have a sincere desire to help those who have been confused by their previous study and those who need to organize their thinking in this field. Since at least a year of theoretical study is presupposed on the reader's part, no attempt will be made to define terms in common use.

The suggested procedures have been employed with students at the summer sessions of Northwestern University, Roosevelt University, and the University of Michigan; many of them were graduate students who had already done some teaching in the field; others planned to teach. Although any textbook on harmony is presumably "The Way I Teach Harmony,"

Preface

this book is not a text in the usual sense. It summarizes teaching methods and suggests generalizations which have proved useful. All of these methods have been tested in my teaching of undergraduates at Denison University. I have also observed the teaching of theory in a considerable number of institutions. A great variety of methods is in use; some of these are effective and some are of doubtful value. A number of procedures observed have been exceedingly wasteful of the students' time. With the great expansion in the field of harmony in the twentieth century, it is all the more imperative that we cover the conventions of older practice as speedily and efficiently as possible. To bring this about, integration and generalization will be used wherever possible in this book.

The observation of as many teachers as possible and the reading of many different texts are important to the teacher, for the ideas which a good teacher uses come from many different sources. To acknowledge my indebtedness here would be to list all the teachers and many students I have known, as well as the authors of a bibliography much more extensive than the one which accompanies this book. It is my hope that you in turn will find here some ideas of value and use.

Denison University
November 1959

TABLE OF CONTENTS

First Things First

WHEN it comes to placing first things first we set up objectives in their order of importance for our work. We want to be informal and avoid stilted language as far as possible, but we should not try to avoid what is meant by the term objective. What do we hope to accomplish in the study of musical theory?

The term "Theory" of music is unfortunate in its connotations. Actually, the theoretical is the most practical approach; the practice of thinking and making music is what we have in mind. If the student senses that he is growing in ability to think and create music, if we can show him that theory saves him a great deal of time in reading music, in memorizing music, in hearing and understanding music (and do this without telling him so), we are succeeding. He must discover these facts for himself although we should be able to demonstrate them. As he grows in ability, he will not read notes or letters but harmonies or words, and as his understanding of theory grows he will not read single chords but well-known progressions or even complete phrases which recur in a given style. One of the differences between the elementary student reading a composition and the more artistic performer is that the beginning student treats essential and non-essential notes alike. If we begin early in the course of study to distinguish between the essential vertical columns of harmonic support and the non-essential melodic decoration which we weave around the column or from one column to the next, we are ready for more artistic performance as soloists or conductors, for faster sight-reading and more efficient memorization.

Progressive teaching would list the following objectives in order of importance: (1) creative expression, (2) honest and thorough hearing, (3) realization of theory in performance at the keyboard, (4) a knowledge of conventional grammar and styles of voice-leading, and (5) analysis of musical literature.

First Things First

In the past the last two have often received an unwarranted share of the attention of teachers and students. It is my belief that the choice of the next chord is much more important than the correctness of its grammatical presentation or the niceties of part-writing. These choices and the resulting idea must be the student's and not the teacher's or the text-book's. (Generalizations concerning conventional choices are time-savers and they will be thoroughly discussed in a later chapter; their use is not a contradiction of the position stated here.) Since the student must hear the choice as the succession he desires among thousands of possible choices, the ear seems to deserve first place — but only if it can be trained creatively. Creativity depends upon ability to hear with the inward imagination before there is any outward result or expression. The ear is extremely important; but when ear-training is pursued exclusively, it can be very dull drudgery, running the risk of setting up psychological blocks in the student's mind. Continued pressure, all from the outside, is discouraging, particularly when the student is in competition in a class with others who seem more advanced. Self-expression is needed to counterbalance this bombardment from the outside. If the student will dictate an idea which the teacher is to recognize and notate, the tables are turned and often the student discovers that the teacher has his own problems in hearing and is learning along with the class to improve his own ear. The teacher on the other hand will be more likely to appreciate the difficulties which his students are having. In other words, it is a good idea to ask the students to compose their own ear-training exercises and perform them while the other students and the teacher notate them.

Although ear-training is high on our list, creative expression is still given first place. How this may be done from the beginning in rhythm alone and with rhythm plus melody will be discussed in the next two chapters. Ideas for ear-training at the elementary level will then be suggested. Many texts state the importance of ear-training in their introductions, but few suggest specific methods since, in the rest of the typical book, so many exercises are given for realization in writing that little time is left for the ear-training which the author praises but does not help to secure.

Realization of the actual sound through performance is an objective which must not be overlooked. It is true that the keyboard presents certain difficulties for students who do not use it regularly in performance. There is Hugo Norden's *Harmony and its Application in Violin Playing,* but I know of no text which draws its illustrations primarily from the literature of wind instruments. The melodic approach to harmony does not present insurmountable difficulties. Arpeggios can be used; if they are executed with fair facility something of the harmonic effect will remain in the mind provided the memory places an "ear pedal" upon the succession and recalls it as a simultaneous combination. This is possible for the vocalist as well as the instrumentalist. There is need for more texts using the melodic approach to harmonic feeling. None the less, the piano key-board will remain the most important approach; and if the teacher will limit the tonalities used for the non-pianists to the simpler ones, much can be accomplished without previous experience at the keyboard. An intermediate step between fingerboard and keyboard used by some in elementary work is the "auto-harp"; the greater the variety of instruments used, the better for ear-training and the encouragement of creativity.

The need for harmonic analysis of musical literature has been implied in what was said above concerning sight-reading and memorization. However, there is a danger in giving analysis too large a place in the time allotted to a class, because no amount of analysis can be substituted for the simplest step of creative expression or synthesis. Some analysis is a good thing; and multiple copies of music should be available for inspection on short notice. For beginning work a supply of song books or hymnals can be kept near at hand. It is usually possible in most schools to find a superseded edition which may be useful. Naturally, the quality of this material and its editing should be the criteria for your selection; however, availability is of prime importance and this material should probably be left in the classroom for quick distribution. Later, music which the student is studying in his applied music should be used for special sessions of analysis.

If analysis is to serve the objective of ear-training it should also be done without the printed score. The work of fellow students can be used for this purpose. Responses from each student by the use of various hand-signs will be suggested later. At this point I merely wish to emphasize the fact that short aural responses are much better than written-out analyses of notes in columns, their roots deduced without recognition of the actual sound. Many students can analyze in a mechanical fashion, labelling a harmony with correct Roman numeral, inversion, alterations and all that without realizing that they have before them a famous cliché or an effect which they have heard frequently in the romantic music of the nineteenth century or in songs at the last student recital. The sound of the double dissonance of the "French Augmented Sixth" or the menacing effect

[8]

of the lowered sixth in the borrowed chords of the parallel minor scale can be recognized and given a "nickname" much more quickly than its source and numerical alterations can be listed (as Franklin W. Robinson points out in his *Aural Harmony*).

There is always opportunity to demonstrate the value of harmonic analysis in memorization. If the teacher, after analyzing a sentence of the music which a student brings to class, can then close the score and give a fairly accurate performance of the music, he will gain at once the student's respect for the methods used in analysis and for the analytical process in general.

The location of analysis in the last place on our list of objectives is not in accord with the emphasis placed upon it in the theories of Heinrich Schenker, which continue the process of analyzing the first analysis and so on in layers of structures, the *reductio ad absurdum* of which is a single triad for the whole composition. Of course, Schenker's belief that the number of harmonies in a given piece of music is much smaller than was supposed has great value as a contrast to the totalling of every column of notes like a column of figures. In some institutions harmonic analysis is taught as a separate course; however, a thorough understanding of the field of harmony should bring with it analysis as an easy and natural accompaniment at every stage of the work. The feeble and humble self-expression of the student is more important than any amount of analysis.

Knowledge of conventional grammar and voice-leading has been placed near the end of our list of objectives. There was a time when this was given the greatest emphasis by teachers, almost to the exclusion of other objectives. Its present position in the thinking of progressive teachers may be in part a reaction to this former over-emphasis; it is also a recognition of freedom and the many changes from orthodoxy in the styles of contemporary composers. Probably the disregard in recent music of the principles of voice-leading is more apparent than real. The present is a contrapuntal period in many respects and the methods of voice-leading in conventional harmony afford a natural basis of regularity upon which to build. Although it is not high in our list of objectives the grammar of a musical sentence must not be neglected.

It is true that the conventions of harmony are still subject to change and in fact the rate of change seems to be accelerated in our day. This may be an illusion, as Hindemith points out in his *Craft of Musical Composition* when he quotes Fux to the effect that composers were refusing to be bound by any rules or principles. (Fux was writing during the lifetime of Bach and Handel!) Every age has witnessed changes in this living language of music just as it has seen them in spoken languages. Although the theory of music should not spend too much time on the strict conventions of an older period, the musician needs to be thoroughly familiar with them. Certain methods of connection, logically very simple, form the background of the period of common practice (approximately 1600-1900) in text books devoted to part-writing; they can be mastered very quickly, leaving the student to concentrate his attention upon those situations which may be less conventional. Regularity of treatment in what we will call the regular conjugations then serves as the basis for explorations in style. In his own analysis of the literature that he is performing, the student should be aware of the unusual as a deviation from the regular. It is an excellent idea at this point to show Brahms' own notebook containing the illustrations of parallel fifths which he found in the music he read. This is published in a facsimile edition by the Universal Edition. (The fact that the reproduction shows clearly that Brahms used for a second time music paper he had used for other purposes and erased, probably because this was an item of expense he had to watch at this time in his life, may remind your students to count their blessings.) Students should be urged to keep note-books in ink of their own work, including interesting illustrations they have discovered. The copying of music is good for the inner ear or imagination, and in some ways early composers were fortunate if they had to copy scores because printed copies were not available; or if they had to play from full score because they did not have phonograph records to do that for them. In some respects the earlier handicaps were blessings in disguise.

We have reviewed briefly the five objectives of any good course in theory; these will be given detailed treatment in later chapters. However, the best teaching combines these objectives in various ways and keeps all students active throughout the class in one way or another. A few possibilities for this integrated type of session can be mentioned here. While one student is playing or singing his own rhythmic or melodic ideas, all the others should be busy recognizing or reproducing these choices upon individual keyboards or at the blackboard. Questions from the teacher to those not directly under his observation will keep the other students alert and interested. When this is done the first three objectives listed above are covered simultaneously, although the students who have not made the initial choices are receiving only ear-training and keyboard-training. When only one piano is available in the classroom, inexpensive cardboard-keyboards may be purchased and placed on each desk. There is more expensive equipment which has certain advantages if cost does not have to be considered. Keyboards with the black keys raised give the feeling of the chords as at a real keyboard. Still more expensive keyboards have keys which move, and the most expensive equipment produces sound for the teacher and the student. I have found the inexpensive diagrams of the keyboard quite satisfactory if the class is not too large and if the teacher or his student-assistants can circulate behind the seats of those using the keyboards. Since dictation with sustained sound is a good idea, possibly an inexpensive harmonium or a reed organ may be found to provide an additional keyboard. Varying the medium of dictation by use of wind or string instruments is also an excellent idea.

Our fourth and fifth objectives should be constantly associated with each other and with the second and third. Analysis of music should often be done through the ear even if questions concerning part-writing may need to refer to printed music for analysis. For instance, if a student is inclined to use irregular resolutions of the dominant seventh all the time, ask him to find in, say, a hymnal, illustrations of the way he is handling these chords. By the time he has found his method of treatment he will know the

[13]

meaning of "irregularity" as "one in ten times" or even as "one in a hundred." Regular then means "as a rule" and not "a rule which must always be obeyed." Sight-singing and ear-training combine with creative expression when a student sings the melody he, or one of his fellows, has just written while the teacher watches the manuscript to see that the notation agrees. Other students at the same time may write and later sing the same thing. The result is an integrated lesson.

One can teach theory with little or no equipment; however, more efficient teaching can be done if you have enough space for the entire class at blackboards with painted or indented musical staves. If this is not available it is possible to purchase blackboards which may be hung like pictures on a wall or supported on easels. Movable chairs with tablet arms are best. They can then be arranged in a circle or in some formation which gives the teacher access to the work of any student not at a blackboard or instrument. Each student should have an inexpensive a-440 pitch-pipe. Whether a text is used or not is relatively unimportant; it is a time-saver for assignments to be completed outside of class but it should never be used exclusively or slavishly. A good teacher can use any text provided he knows how to supplement it with activities of the type suggested in this book.

First Things First

If recording equipment is available many records or tapes should be prepared for use as "unknowns" in ear-training, just as a teacher of chemistry or geology gives the students certain "unknowns" to identify. It seems strange that the musician who needs to train his ear does not find available and ready for his use the type of commercial recordings which are used so much in the teaching of foreign languages. There is a great need for such records to be used in a laboratory for listening. A beginning has been made in the recordings of the Rutgers Series produced under the direction of A. Kunrad Kvam and published by the Music Minus One Company. Until many others are available you will need to manufacture your own for assignments. Too often the training of the ear continues only when the teacher is present to dictate.

A projectoscope is another very useful piece of equipment as it will throw a student's written work directly upon a wall or screen so that all may see it as it is discussed or may perform it as an ensemble. Even a chamber-music group or a small orchestra can perform from the image of a score enlarged on such a screen. This is a great time-saver for the teacher who otherwise must copy on the board the work which is being discussed. Some of the worst teaching I have observed has been done when a teacher was playing one student's work at the piano with all the others crowded around, their attention and interest diminishing by the square of the distance from the manuscript. If he does not have a projectoscope, the teacher should copy at least pertinent sections of the students' work, if possible in advance of the class.

There is no possibility of avoiding considerable labor outside the class-hour, and the teacher who tries to do so will not make the best use of the opportunities presented in class. Homework, if assigned, should be read and criticized outside class with written comments which are complete and thoroughly intelligible. Then only a limited selection of typical errors and suggestions need be discussed in the actual class. Too often the courses are taught by people whose primary interests are elsewhere, teachers of applied music or other subjects who seem to want to get all their work done in the classroom. This is not to say that there are no good teachers who thus divide their interests, and certainly a teacher of applied music should be able to "apply" theory as well. However, if there is division of responsibility for theory among a number of people, for all of whom it is a secondary interest, there is danger that it will be poorly taught. Possibly some of the ill-repute of theory results from such teaching.

First Things First

The conventions of musical notation need some attention, for they actually save time in performance as well as in writing. Tonality still has its demands for logical spelling, and the notation which saves an accidental is usually better. Everything which the teacher places before the student should be "ready for the printer" and this objective should be kept before the class. One of the best demonstrations that anything less than conventional notation is a waste of time may occur in the classroom when a fellow student has difficulty in understanding another's notation or there is a delay for the addition of necessary accidentals. The pertinent remark: "If you were paying your performers union wages this would cost you considerable money for lost time," is effective!

CHAPTER II

Beginning with Rhythm

I N the beginning rhythm is all you need. Little in the way of material is needed for the first steps in composition. If students begin by composing or improvising rhythms they will seek notation for the sake of a permanent record or for communication of ideas and instructions to performers. The theory of rhythmic notation can be explained gradually as it is needed. The ears of the listeners must answer the questions: Where are the accents? How large is the measure? Where are the punctuations between phrases? Are these phrases alike in size or are they irregular?

Beginning with Rhythm

If Vincent d'Indy's idea, expressed in his *Cours de Composition* and in his teaching at the Schola Cantorum, has validity and we should retrace the history of the art in our teaching, then rhythm is the logical point of beginning for that is where primitive peoples begin to express themselves musically. A teacher in this field will have to be a pioneer. Compared with the many volumes written concerning harmony, there are few indeed devoted to the composition of melody and still less has been written about rhythm. However, creative expression must not be postponed and if you begin by demanding rhythms from your students they will soon lose their feeling of self-consciousness and grow in confidence even to the point of audacity.

It is a good idea to have at hand drums of various sizes and other types of percussion, but if they are not available clapping the hands or striking objects in the room will serve. Once students discover the joy of self-expression they will not cease creating. The longer we delay in encouraging this, the more difficult it will become; the first time we meet students we should ask them to say something in music rhythmically. The objection may be raised that rhythms without at least some melodic inflection do not constitute music. Regardless of your answer to that theoretical or semantic question, there is no doubt that self-expression is fundamentally rhythmic. With the many things to be accomplished in the two years of beginning musical theory in college, we cannot afford to devote as much time to pure rhythm as we might like to give. Soon the setting of words in rhythm should be begun and soon thereafter the addition of melody is advisable. Fortunate indeed are those students who have been encouraged to express themselves rhythmically in secondary and elementary classes in music, physical education and the dance. Rhythm should continue to be a part of all future courses in music. Too many harmony exercises have been deficient in rhythmic interest. They may be useful reductions or condensations of the main voice-leadings but they need to unfold and extend in actual rhythmic life. The Germans have a word for it: "Auskomponierung." The influence of one harmony may extend over several measures in rhythmic and melodic life before there is in reality a change to another harmony.

Do not look down upon rhythmic composition as the equivalent of finger-painting in the visual arts. The rhythmic aspect of a musical idea is always more than half of the vitality and personality of the idea; this fraction is indeed much larger in contemporary music where rhythm is often the main basis of organization. To demonstrate that recognition of an idea depends upon rhythm, try beating

Beginning with Rhythm

the rhythm of some song which your students know; before you are through several will have recognized it. "Dixie" is a good one to use. It is always recognized when rhythm alone is given but if you first take the pitches of "Dixie" and alter the rhythms radically no one will recognize the result. Far from being a childish approach, work in rhythm alone may be extended to cover almost the entire field of composition. Isadore Freed had a course at the college level (Hartt College of Music) based upon rhythm without melody, which covered an entire year. All the principles of unity and variety, punctuation and cadence, Bergson's *élan vital, épanouissement et chute* or initial idea, development to climax followed by falling action, may be discussed in terms of rhythm. Any of the musical forms including the sonata form and fugue can be realized.

Monotony as a result of primitive repetition of the same rhythm has a certain fascination for the savage or indeed for the composer, but variety which goes to the other extreme and lacks any basis of organization also has its delights and its dangers. Chaos can be just as monotonous for the listener as unrelieved repetition. All these problems can be discussed in terms of your students' work in rhythm, as examples both of too much unity and of too little are likely to appear. Thus, at this level and with only the simplest material, the most important problems of musical art can be discussed and solutions attempted. If we wait until a student has all the technique he really needs before we begin composition, he will never start because the acquisition of such a technique is a lifelong quest. Those who teach aural recognition discover that rhythms are as difficult to recognize as differences in pitch if not more difficult. It is well to begin early with this important phase of music.

I would also like to emphasize the very personal satisfaction which comes from rhythmic self-expression. It is so closely related to eurhythmics or the rhythm of life itself that a student's personality may "blossom out" with a little encouragement in a way that gives particular pleasure. This has long been recognized by the followers of Dalcroze (who was also a composer, by the way) and by others in the field of physical education and the dance. Compositions performed with a few simple instruments, possibly improvised ones, or solely by hand-clapping will have added interest if interpreted by dancers. When percussion instruments of different timbres and apparent pitches are used we are already on our way to melody. One of the best suggestions you could give your students at this point would be that they cooperate with the department of esthetic dancing or

Beginning with Rhythm

"modern dance," assisting in creative improvisation and providing music for their sessions. A number of professional dancers use percussion only as the musical accompaniment. You will find the teachers of dance primarily interested in rhythm, and if the student uses a group of fingers or his fists at the keyboard to produce the sound in tone-clusters they will not object.

The examples appended to this chapter were contributed by entering college students, but similar results could be secured not only in high school but from much earlier age groups. Ex. 1 suffers from too much unity. You can suggest consideration of the classical principle that "the third time something should happen." More often, however, the compositions have too much variety or enough ideas for half-a-dozen pieces. When there is no reference in the second half of a statement to any idea from the first half (ex. 2), immediate repetition, with some slight change as antithesis produces a more satisfactory form. Even so slight an addition as that of one eighth note to ex. 1 improved ex. 3.

Generally the size of the first small rhythmic unit should be made clear to the audience by repetition. The further we go in a musical sentence the more continuous the style may be. Very often a compound structure is used in which the opening of the answering phrase is similar to the opening of the first statement, as in the sentence: "If it is a fine day we may have a picnic; but if it is not such a fine day we may have to stay at home." The conclusion of the second half of the compound sentence may or may not be similar to the conclusion of the first half. There are many possibilities. The sentences need not be regular and the teacher should hesitate to condemn irregularity if any logical basis can be found for its defense (ex. 4-5). If the student can remember and repeat accurately a complex statement, that in itself is strong evidence for its validity.

The above will give some idea of what may be done at the elementary level. We will meet all of these problems again when we add a melodic contour and discuss the location of the climax, open and closed structures and the necessity of keeping the form open until the close by relativity of cadence. The lure of the subtle and the irregular, provided it is intelligible, appears in self-expression even on the simplest level. At a more advanced level, part-writing may be represented by rhythm alone. The "Geographic Fugue" of Ernest Toch (published in the *New Music Quarterly,* "Fuge aus Geographie") uses a speaking chorus or quartet and presents the names of places in rhythms to reproduce all the features of a fugue. This was made even more obvious in a taped performance at double or quadruple speed. Much of the music of Bartok, Stravinsky and other modern composers uses rhythm as the main basis of organization.

Beginning with rhythm and with that alone in the theory class may seem to some a violation of a principle enunciated by psychologists: present wholes, not parts. Mursell, for instance, states, "Do not separate the elements of music and never separate time and tone; present music as a whole and not in its component parts." Such a statement refers in the main to the study, reading, analysis or performance of music already containing many facets. We can defend our composition in rhythms by emphazing the fact that the result *is* Music, with a capital M. The result is the *whole* expression; it is a living organization and it is an expression of the whole personality of the composer. How true this is throughout musical style! The rhythms of Poulenc in his Quintet for piano and woodwinds are definitely French, even more narrowly Parisian and in Paris, the apotheosis of rhythms found in the Boulevard café or in the Vaudeville. The rhythms of our American composers are definitely American. Nothing seems more personal than rhythmic self-expression. I have seen a student's work present features not only of his own generation and country but those of ancestry from a foreign country even when the student, in one case, was a third generation American.

You learn a great deal about your students from their rhythmic compositions. If the imagination of the student needs stimulation at this point or at any later stage, there is no reason why the suggestion of a "program" and title should not be tried. Titles such as a game of tennis (*Jeux,* Debussy) of a football game (*Rugby,* Honegger) have not been beneath the dignity of composers; any title which suggests movement may be used. Words with rhythm help although their addition presents a number of problems. They may be used with rhythms only, at this point in the course, in two ways: (1) the student may be asked to make up words to fit the idea which he has already composed in rhythm, or (2) he may be asked to suggest rhythms for words assigned in advance. The first is a little easier than the second provided you do not insist upon rhymes or literary value. If the words fit the rhythms well, you know that the student is hearing the music correctly before it has been performed. If necessary he may clap the rhythm, since this may suggest words as pronounced by some character in a cartoon-film. Be satisfied if there is a good correspondence of words with rhythms. In the setting of words by others it is wise to begin with poetry which is fairly regular;

then proceed from that to the more subtle and finally to the setting of prose. One of the good features in Murphy and Stringham's *Creative Harmony and Musicianship** is the printing of a large number of poems arranged somewhat in the order of rhythmic difficulty. The words for examples Nos. 6-8 are taken from this book with permission of the authors. At first it may help to have students read the words and underscore the important words or syllables and then suggest: "Turn up the underscoring on the left end of each mark and you will get possible and good locations for barlines," which is only another way of saying that the important accents usually come right after the barlines.

The notation of rhythms is not always easy, but the student's need to remember his work from one day to the next or to prepare it for performance by others will motivate him and train him in accuracy and the need for mastery of a technique. If we as teachers are writing down the ideas of a student we must be careful not to change them in that process. Respect the student's insistence that his idea has merit or that the notation has not yet captured his intent. Ask that his performance be a strong and deliberate one and note particularly if he can repeat it accurately. Have

*Howard Ansley Murphy and Edwin John Stringham, *Creative Harmony and Musicianship*: An Introduction to the Structure of Music (New York: Prentice-Hall, 1951).

the other students help with their criticisms and also check on the accuracy of the repetitions.

Throughout your work with students it is wise, so far as possible, to demand that they perform their own compositions. This quickly tells you whether the music is an intellectual concoction that has been figured out mathematically or whether it is a genuine personal expression which the student knows should sound a certain way. This suggestion should be followed not only when dealing with rhythmic composition but at all other points in melodic and harmonic expression as well. Of course, despite a strong emphasis upon creativity we must assure our students that we are really not trying to train a class of composers any more than the English Department is primarily training poets or novelists. The course must be helpful and useful for all musicians. Nevertheless, an imaginative, creative approach produces better results in both English and music and makes the daily work more meaningful for all. It is often the case that the student who is a non-major or who is not at least a performing major shows great originality and should be encouraged. The men often surpass the women in creativity in rhythm. Have you ever wondered why we have no women composers of the first rank? We can scarcely place Chaminade, Dame Ethel Smith, or Mrs. H. H. A. Beach in high posi-

Beginning with Rhythm

tions of the second or third "ranks." Nevertheless the hall of fame in composition has ample space for the woman composer. We should challenge women as well as men to write and keep on writing. At least, let us not discourage creativity in our theory courses even though we realize that few of our students will become composers of prominence.

(i) Too much unity (1)

(ii) Too much variety

(iii) Number one, improved

(iv) Seven measures. Repetition would make a satisfactory 14-measure statement.

(v) Repetition would supply the needed unity.

(vi)   Words by Tennyson

The   splen - dor   falls   on   cas - tle   walls   and

Beginning with Rhythm

snow - y sum-mits old in sto - ry: The

long light shakes a - cross the lakes and the

3
wild cat - a - ract leaps in glo - ry.

(vii)

The splen - dor falls on cas - tle walls and

snow - y sum-mits old in sto - ry: The

long light shakes a - cross the lakes and the

wild cat - a - ract leaps in glo - ry.

(Obviously, this student is less gifted rhythmically than the writers of Nos. vi or viii.)

Teaching Music Theory

(viii)

The splen - dor falls on cas - tle walls and snow - y sum-mits old in sto - ry: The long light shakes a - cross the lakes and the wild cat - a - ract leaps in glo - ry.

[32]

CHAPTER III

Adding Melody

THERE are two principal theories as to the origin of music, one which seeks the origin in rhythm and the other which looks for it in excited speech and melody derived from that. The evolution of melody from rhythm seems more logical than an evolution from speech to rhythm. If we beat a rhythm on a resonant object, the top of the piano for instance, it almost seems as if the accents are themselves higher in pitch; it is also quite natural for the voice in speaking to rise at that point which coincides with an added physical exertion or accent. Regardless of these theories, the addition of melody cannot long be postponed in the education of a musician. Melody is enhanced by rhythm; in fact, we cannot think of melody without rhythm. Rhythms already composed cry for variations in pitch. It is not necessary to assemble harmonic vocabulary before we begin. Let us see what we can do with two notes of different pitch:

(2)

The relation between thesis and antithesis is obvious. Then try three:

(3)

Adding Melody

Next increase the range to four, using students' work for sight-singing and dictation:

(4)

Five notes, C to G, of course increase the possibilities immensely:

(5)

It is a good idea to demonstrate that a five-note range need not produce a conventional result. Stravinsky's *Les cinq doits,* in which he uses the five fingers in fixed positions on the white notes of the piano, shows that what is modern in the music depends not so much upon the given materials as upon the way in which they are used.

We have seen in connection with rhythm that important principles of form can be taught with rhythms alone. The same principles apply in melody. Monotony results when primitive repetition is carried to excess, and a very similar monotony may result from too much variety. When the listener cannot sense some unity in the variety and ceases to try to do so, the result is just as monotonous as the mesmeric effect of repeated rhythms. Chaos is monotonous. Each note

Adding Melody

must be about its master's business. I am reminded of a remark made by Ernest Bloch at a session of the Ohio Music Teachers Association: "I can teach all of composition from the first eight measures of the first Beethoven Piano Sonata." After hearing him talk for an hour on these eight measures, one was ready to agree with his statement.

While harmonic change is not necessary at this point in composition, it is a good idea to place underneath the melody, for the purposes of performance, an open fifth. This fifth may be sustained, as so often occurs in instruments such as the bagpipe and the hurdy-gurdy, or the pattern of the single fifth may be varied rhythmically. The two notes of the fifth may be used in various patterns:

(6)

These patterns of course point to the fact that the open fifth can imply two harmonies, the tonic and the dominant; but we are already anticipating the next chapter. The accompaniment of the fifth suggests certain national or folk styles, Scotch, Amerindian, etc.; the melodies can be diatonic or chromatic and may be simple or as complex as the student wishes — as Oriental in the arabesque of ornamentation as our duodecuple scale permits.

Rhythms composed earlier in class can be performed in scale-wise melody without skips or repeated notes but with occasional changes of direction. The student will begin to sense the unique character of each scale-degree: the "one-ness of one," or, if you use syllables, the "do-ness of do" and the "la-ness of la." All systems of association have some justification if they call attention to the individual characteristic of each step of the scale-ladder. The shape-notes used in the Sacred Harp Hymnals of the South represent the same kind of association whether seven shapes, or the four shapes showing the double tetrachord-basis of the scale, are used.

Principles of form enter into consideration: it is advisable to keep the form "open" at the middle cadence, avoiding the root or the third at such points in order to create a longer melodic span. The fact that the third is less final than the tonic and leaves the structure more open becomes apparent. The advisability of avoiding too many successive phrase-endings that are alike either melodically or rhythmically can be discussed. Bartok's *Mikrokosmos,* Vol. II, No.

Adding Melody

40, and other illustrations can be played to show that great composers often write, with very simple means, works of real self-expression and artistry.

Words should be set to melodies at this point in the course. They may be added to melodies already written provided we do not insist that the words supplied have literary merit and are content if they merely agree in accent and inflection. Setting poetry or prose by important writers develops taste and emphasizes the fact that the musician needs a sympathetic understanding of the other arts. Students who are having difficulty with rhythm in performance are discovered by such assignments and may be helped to solve their problems. Conversely, a famous teacher of piano, Artur Schnabel, often improvised words to fit the rhythms and thus improve the phrasing of his students' performances.

Even with only the three notes C, D, and E the sensitive student discovers the finality of C, the modality of D and E, the questioning character of E, the feeling of half-satisfaction on D, etc. If we substitute D, E, and F, we find the middle note still modal in feeling, but what a different mode! The major-final is now on top. The choice of C, C♯ and D, or B, C, D and E, F, G lends variety to melodic writing with three notes. With the four notes F, G, A, B there is, of course, a great increase in the number of possibilities. Hindemith in his *Elementary Training for Musicians* forces the student to enter the twentieth century by his use of these four notes in the early chapters for ear-training and sight-singing. Many of them are quite unusual, for it is almost impossible to suggest with these notes a ruling major mode. The Lydian with F as 1, the Mixolydian with G as 1, the Aeolian with A as 1, and the Locrian with B as final are possibilities with this section of the whole-tone scale.

In the notation of rhythms alone it is not necessary to use the staff. At the beginning of work with melody a résumé of the development of melodic notation beginning with the neumes may interest your students. For a melody based on three adjacent notes a single straight line is actually all that is needed, for we may place notes above and below the line as well as on it. The pitch of the single line should be given by a letter affording a key to the exact locations of the three notes represented (the word "clef" is "key" in French). With four notes or more, two or more lines help; the Roman Catholic Church still uses a four-line clef in its chant books. More than five lines are a bit confusing; our grand staff of eleven lines uses the middle line only as needed for leger-lines. Other clefs than the F and G clefs should be explained; however, the important thing at this time is preserving the students' ideas in the clef or clefs with which they are most familiar.

Another preliminary method of melodic approach is the composition of "bugle calls." This forces the student to consider the connotational meanings of root, third and fifth. Some of the famous bugle calls may be used for dictation and their symbolism pointed out. The students may have returned from a vacation at a summer camp where specific calls were used for specific purposes — the call to meals, the call for swimming, etc. Students can be asked to write more arpeggio patterns for specific purposes either without or with words.

It is logical that a combination of arpeggio and scale would follow with skips between the notes of the arpeggio alone and scale-wise treatment elsewhere. Before long, this will seem a mechanical limitation and the student should be given complete melodic freedom as soon as he seems ready for it. All types of melodic decoration will occur. Melodies can be written with appoggiaturas above and below all chord tones, both a half-step and a whole step away. When the diatonic appoggiaturas are combined we get the flavor of non-tonic harmony as in the alternate chord of a mouth-organ. The relationships of such an effect can be sung melodically: B, d, d, c, f, e, a, g, b, c'.

Compared with the many volumes written on harmony there has been little said about the composition of melody. While little can be said, much can be done. It is better to ask for melody and accept what you get than to prescribe and circumscribe in advance. The reader may be interested in my discussion of Prout's "impossible" melody* which indicates that his collection of pitches is much less radical than many melodies written today. Melody is that which is accepted by the hearer as melody; this circular definition means that the organization takes place in the listener's mind and depends upon his punctuation for definition. The idea of what constitutes melody is now so enlarged that a teacher should hesitate to throw into the wastebasket any student's melody merely because of irregularity, angularity, lack of unity or superficial imbalance. Watch for strong self-expression, for the will to sing or perform the melody; and be thankful for creativity, which may take unusual directions. The normal and regular will be demonstrated with the appearance of familiar cadences:

(7)

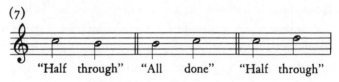

"Half through"   "All   done"   "Half   through"

*Karl H. Eschman, *Changing Forms in Modern Music*, E. C. Schirmer Music Co., Boston, 1945, p. 50.

Adding Melody

"All done" "A - men"

It is good practice to have these sung beginning with the same pitch, as this trains the feeling for modulation:

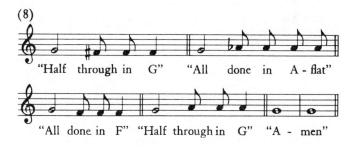

"Half through in G" "All done in A - flat"

"All done in F" "Half through in G" "A - men"

A wide range of styles will appear. Problems of musical notation will have to be solved as they arise. Conventional spelling versus unconventional accidentals will appear in chromatic sections. "Ready to print" should be an objective. Be quick to recognize the possibilities of the unusual, the beauty of the irregular and the strength of the angular. Melodic decoration is a natural instinct. If there is any justification for the student's complaint that theoretical exercises are not like music, it is because the use of embellishments and their discussion is often left to the final lessons of a course instead of serving from the start as a creative stimulus. Composition of melodies early in the course is a good answer to this justifiable criticism.

The following typical illustrations were handed in during the first week of theory in college:

Adding Melody

accompaniment continues **ad. lib.**

Adding Melody

(c)

(accompaniment continues)

Teaching Music Theory

CHAPTER IV

Training the Ear

BEFORE going further in this discussion of theory in the education of a musician, let us consider in more detail the training of his "ear," which has already been placed high upon the list of objectives in any course. To begin, suggest that each student purchase a pitch-pipe or a tuning-fork and try to sing its pitch each morning before he has heard any music. Suggest that he make this as much a habit as the brushing of his teeth. A single-pitch (a-440) pipe can be purchased for less than fifty cents and will prove to be of great value. If it were necessary for him to sing a good a-440 to get his breakfast every morning, or to sing C if he wanted grapefruit and E-flat if he wanted an orange, he would soon acquire that ability. A student must realize that ability to hear has a direct bearing upon his success in music, in fact upon the income he may have for fruit of any kind! His own performance and his training of others' performances depend upon the accuracy of his hearing. No organization is better than the ear of its director. This ability, then, is important for the non-composer as well as for the composer.

While absolute pitch is not a prerequisite for success in music, striving for absolute pitch improves the ability to recognize relative pitches. This helps to "focus" the ear and to bring attention to bear upon the particular sound or sounds rather than upon the more vague general effect. Whatever the psychologists may say about the inheritance of absolute pitch or about the fact that it seems to be a "gift" in some cases (I have known one of these cases, a person of subnormal ability in every other respect), it is my belief based upon experience that a fairly reliable sense of absolute pitch can be acquired in a reasonably short time if regular attention is given to it. Make your improvement a hobby and be pleased with your successes, which will increase in frequency. There will be a feeling of personal growth and of greater artistic integrity or honesty as well as efficiency when the ability to hear accurately improves. Of course, there is scarcely any limit to the challenges presented to the ear in this field, particularly in the complicated combinations of modern music. As a teacher, ask your students to report whether they tried for the pitch on their pitch-pipe before entering the classroom. Ask them, if they did not succeed, whether they are, as a rule, too high or too low. Their grades should not be lowered for failure to sing the pitch but only for failure to make the attempt. The questions should be asked at every session for a while and then at irregular intervals.

If you have a piano, keep it tuned to a-440. It is a good idea to ask your students to stand with their backs to a piano keyboard, strike a very high or very low pitch, and then try to match it in their own singing range. By turning around and bringing the note down by octaves into this register they can check their success without the help of a teacher.

There have been many attempts to fix colors which may be associated with each tonality; but the tables provided by various authors do not agree. If you happen to think in terms of color that Bb is a brassy yellow, Eb orange, F major blue, or D major green, that may be of some use to you but it will not help me. Regardless of such questionable association, there can be no doubt that there is a

"C-majorishness" about the tonality of C major, and a differing and individual character about each of the other major and minor tonalities. This may be dependent upon the location of the finals in the vocal register or upon some other factor; whatever the causes, which theorists have debated, of the differences, the fact that each tonality has its own "personality" remains. Hindemith discusses the reasons for his selection of certain keys in the preface to the second version of his song-cycle *Das Marienleben*. Seize upon the personal flavor of each key and try to recognize it; if associations help, use them as well. Whether you are a student or a teacher needing more reliable and accurate hearing, the following suggestions may prove useful. If you have a radio, allow it to dictate to you: ask yourself the tonality of the music you are hearing, and if you have a piano in the same room, test your decision by playing the tonal center or keynote of the music you are hearing on the air. If the organ or piano in your school or church is also at a-440, try to decide the tonality of a hymn or song used for the assembly before you open the book to see if you are correct.

There are many ways in which the ear can be trained. We are fortunate today because we have so much music presented to us by phonograph and radio or television. I am quite certain that the sense of good intonation is much more nearly accurate in our students today than it was when I began my teaching. Whatever we may think about the artistic value of much of the music that comes to us over the air or on records, at least we can say that most studio pianos are in tune and that most soloists or organizations have to use fairly good intonation to stay in business. If you have a recording machine, use it to prepare records containing "unknowns" which your students can hear and try to identify. The difficulty of using complete compositions as they come to you on the air is that they are too difficult and move too rapidly for beginning drill. Students can be asked to analyze your simpler recordings as they would an unknown in chemistry or geology and their answers may be graded by an assistant or a helper who need not even be a musician. If you report to the student only the percentage of his success or failure in identifying what is on the record, the entire list of correct answers is not so likely to become common property of the class.

If you play any instrument, try to hear the composition you play when you are away from the instrument, and try to hear it in the key in which you perform it. This is not too difficult since you will have repeated the music many times as you were learning it; the ear has a good memory which will improve if you persist in recalling the way your performance sounds. In fact, many people say that absolute pitch is only the result of memory from one day to the next. Along this same line, associate certain well-known and frequently heard pieces with their respective keys; for instance: "The Star-Spangled Banner" with B♭ major; "My country, 'tis of thee" with F major; the "Doxology" with G major, etc.

The development of a good ear by hearing music in the inner imagination can be of great use in memorization of music for public performance. It is true that this is a field of application somewhat outside the usual range of the harmony classroom; however, the more uses we can find for our teaching the more benefits we confer and the better our teaching will be. If the students of your class are to be won over, two things must happen: (1) your student must experience and realize an improvement in his ability in some direction: in ears, fingers, mind, etc., and (2) he must discover that theoretical training is valuable in his other activities, not in some far-distant future, but now, while he is studying. If he knows he is improving and if he can see for himself the value of what he is doing, he will be cooperative and interested for the entire course, and his gratitude will increase as the years go by. So I would urge you to try the experiment of playing or singing an entire composition which you have memorized, *"in your head."* This may seem at present too difficult for you, but make the attempt! If you can do it for the first two measures of a composition, you can do it for the entire composition and eventually for an entire program. Then you will be in a position to urge your students to do the same; if you play in public, you can testify to the many resources which this adds in performance. It will be hard work but with practice it becomes easier and it is worth all the effort it costs. To say nothing of what it will do for your mental ear, you will discover that it doubles every memory which you have and gives you twice as many resources at the time of public performance. Actually you have been playing or singing with a number of memories: your fingers and your throat or lips have memories of their own; there are also melodic, harmonic and rhythmic memories. They are often so generalized in your consciousness that they are not as helpful as they can be when focused and made more definite. A melody comes to you but you hear it without thinking of its exact pitches; this is not enough. You will feel much more secure in public performance when all the memories you have been using more or less unconsciously in the past have been doubled by some conscious practice in the mind or imaginative ear.

[55]

Teaching Music Theory

You will find that one hour of such practice will produce the results of several hours of work with your instrument. This is possible because technical difficulties are fundamentally mental difficulties. When a passage is cleared up mentally its performance is facilitated physically. On the day of your recital you can go through your program out-of-doors or in pleasant surroundings, exercising your imaginary muscles. In fact, with this kind of practicing almost everything happens except the overt motion; the commands of the mind reach almost to the finger-tips or the lips and yet the actual muscles are not tired. You can perform with an inner "honesty" of musicianship which makes you much more secure. And I hope that you, as a teacher of theory, *will* perform. It is not good for teachers of theory to become too divorced from the rest of the world of music makers. The performance may be only in your classroom but it should demonstrate that you are using the methods you teach. Harmonic analysis, which relegates to melodic decoration as much of the detail as possible, may be combined with this type of mental practice.

While recordings illustrating problems in theory are greatly needed and should be manufactured if possible, one can use recordings of the simpler compositions in the classical period for ear-training. Even in these the changes of harmony and tonality may seem to occur so rapidly and so frequently that the student at first will complain that the music is too difficult to analyze by ear. He should be satisfied first with recognition of the most important changes in tonality, for instance, the key of the second subject in the sonata forms of the classical period. Often the key of the composition or at least its first movement is stated on the program and the related keys used in the composition confined to the right and left neighbors of its musical world. A knowledge of the "whole world" as represented in the following circle of fifths is presupposed:

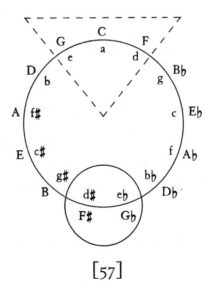

[57]

(The order used coincides with the clockwise progressions of the first conjugation, introduced in Chapter VI.)

If you take a segment of this circle such as that indicated by the dotted lines, containing six keys, the middle major tonality will represent a center to which the other five keys are related; similarly those related to the central minor tonality will be the remaining five. This visual relationship is probably easier to remember than the statement that the related keys of any given major (or minor) tonality are its dominant and subdominant together with the relative minors (or majors) of all three keys. Be sure that your students are as familiar with the bottom of this musical world as they are with the top. It is more useful to think enharmonically beyond six accidentals since tonalities of eight or more sharps or flats waste time, although keys of seven sharps and seven flats need to be explained.

There are two tonalities which are most frequently used as the second important tonal center in a classical composition: the dominant and the relative major. If the main key is major, the tonality usually chosen is the dominant major; if the main tonality is minor, the most likely tonality is the relative major. Supplied with this information, one should try to recognize in the movements of a string quartet, sonata or symphony by Haydn or Mozart which of the two journeys has taken place. Even the more complicated style of the Bach Suites may be used for this purpose if the first half of a movement uses these first choices as goals. At what point in each case has the new key been established? If you are hearing a performance, is the player repeating the first part or is he going on to the second part to make the return trip from the new key? These and other questions are excellent for ear-training. In the field of form, recognition through the ear is much more important than analysis of the score through the eye, so often used exclusively.

We need to recognize that tonalities are the important "floor-levels" in musical architecture. In such a long and complicated symphonic poem as Strauss's *Heldenleben* we find the "hero" in E♭ major in the exposition, with the heroine, the future Mrs. Strauss, on the sharp-side of the circle in E and A majors (solo violin); the end of the exposition of the sonata form is in G♭ or F♯ major, which might be called a compromise, both flat and sharp, at the end of the "first Act." While the music presents a great deal of modulation which will be difficult for students to follow, the important levels of the structure can be clearly heard and the student will be training his sense of tonality, his tonal memory, if he will try to find by ear the return of the "hero" in his home key at the beginning of the recapitulation. Any other work in sonata form can be used for the same purpose. The better your ear, the better your recognition and enjoyment of musical forms. At first, be satisfied with the recognition of near neighbors; with the ear, the slightest success is a cause for rejoicing.

In this, as in other parts of his study, a student must not be surprised to find in his experience what the psychologists call plateaus, where he seems to be making little progress; but if he persists, a new advance will follow later. What happens outside the periods of instruction is even more important than what goes on in the classroom. There is no substitute for thinking music or even "dreaming" music. The would-be musician should live and breathe in a musical world throughout the day and not depend upon "speaking French only in the classroom," to use a parallel situation. When a student can find another student who will "talk music" (not talk *about* music) in a giving and taking of dictation, this is excellent. To supplement this, use recorded materials. When you have no machine or person to dictate to you, sit down in a comfortable chair and hear in your imagination some choir or group of people singing something you know quite well — possibly a folk-song, a patriotic piece, or a hymn. Try to hear all the details and analyze the melody and harmony; if necessary, play the first chord, try energetically to hear the second, check its correctness, and continue; in the case of the melody try singing the numbers of the scale which fit. Or, take a collection of folk-music or a hymnal and read silently in your imagination, first those you know well and then less familiar ones; finally attempt some you cannot remember ever having heard. To prove that you are actually hearing harmonies, try singing them in arpeggio fashion; the notes do not have to be in the same octaves as in the original version. For instance, a well-known hymn might be sung as follows:

(10) The pitches encircled are the notes of the melody.

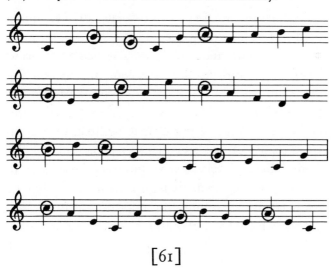

When singing harmonies by arpeggios do not hesitate to run up and down the notes several times with increasing speed after you feel sure of the pitches, trying to put a "pedal" on your memory so that the harmonic combination is felt as an entity. If necessary, test your result at a piano. Again, select some song and write it from memory; then compare it with the printed version. A gradual improvement of ability, in spite of occasional setbacks which are to be expected, will give you increased satisfaction and confidence.

As teachers we need to recognize our own limitations in hearing and we should not attempt to conceal them from our students. If we stay behind the cardboard keyboards in the classroom and not behind the piano where a student is producing keyboard harmony with some liberty of choice, we probably will be forced to improve our own recognition by ear, and we certainly cannot and should not prevent the class from knowing exactly how much or how little we hear. A feeling that all in the room, including the teacher, are learning to improve their hearing produces a better relationship of student and teacher.

Training the Ear

Unless the latter is a genius of the first rank he will still have worlds of hearing to conquer, at least in the music of the twentieth century, and it is good for him to know that his own ability to hear fine distinctions is improving. There is entirely too much musical illiteracy in the profession which is not to say that these illiterates are entirely unsuccessful in music. What we mean by these statements is explained by the meaning of the word illiteracy. A man may be a good citizen and a good workman, successful in certain occupations or manipulations, but we call him illiterate if he cannot write down a message he hears over the telephone. Many "musicians" are still in that situation if we substitute a melody for a message.

After the following chapters on the primary triads and the indexing of harmonic vocabulary, further suggestions for the recognition of harmonies will be given. At this point let us return to the recognition of the initial note and interval of a melody. In this connection the use of well-known melodies seems to help:

For the root: the opening of "The Blue Danube Waltz" (J. Strauss)

For the third: the first three notes of the *Messiah* chorus "And the glory"

For the fifth: the opening of the "Star-Spangled Banner"

If the *Messiah* chorus is not familiar, other tunes starting from the third may be used: "Three blind mice" or "Way down upon the Swanee River;" but the three listed above have the advantage of outlining the entire tonic chord in an arpeggio. It is also a good idea to collect a list of melodies which begin elsewhere than on the root, third or fifth of the key.

One of the fundamental problems of the ear is that of intervals. There are two main methods of teaching the recognition of intervals: (1) reference where possible to the interval's place within a chord structure, and (2) reference to the bottom note of the interval as the tonic of a scale. The first method, for instance, refers the minor sixth, e-c, to its location from three up to eight of a major arpeggio; the other method would hear e as tonic and c as lowered sixth or "le" (lay) of a major scale above the e as "do." The teacher should be familiar with both methods. There are disadvantages in each. The effect of a major third from five to seven is quite different from that of one to three: although there are only twelve intervals on the tempered keyboard their effects in actual use are many times twelve. However, the following classification is helpful:

The "empty" or perfect intervals:

The unison, which sounds as one

Training the Ear

The octave, two notes sounding almost as one

The perfect fifth, root to fifth of Major and minor triads, missing note *inside*

The perfect fourth, fifth up to root of Major and minor triads, missing note *outside*

The "lovely" imperfect consonances:

Larger: The Major sixth from fifth up to third of Major triads

The minor sixth from third up to root of Major triads (the missing note is *inside* these larger intervals)

Smaller: The Major third from root up to a third of Major triads, missing note *above*

The minor third from third up to fifth of Major triads, missing note *below*

The dissonant intervals:

Larger: Milder - minor seventh

Harsher - Major seventh, sounding like a mistuned octave

Smaller: Milder - Major second, begins "Chopsticks"

Harsher - minor second, sounds like a mistuned unison

The ambiguous interval:

The diminished fifth or Augmented fourth.

[65]

One may ask a class an interesting question when this last interval is introduced: How many of you hear this interval as tending to expand, and how many hear it as contracting? In this connection the use of the terms augmented and diminished may be explained as the tendency for things that are large to get larger still and those that are small to diminish. The ambiguous nature of this interval is demonstrated when a class divides into two groups, one of which hears the interval getting larger and the other which hears it getting smaller:

(11)

It is possible to associate the opening of some vocal or instrumental melody with each of the intervals with the exception of the ambiguous interval and the descending major seventh, for which I have not been able to find an illustration at the beginning of a melody. Preferably each student should collect his own list. School songs or hymns that are familiar and instrumental pieces in local use are excellent. Familiarity is more important than musical value at this point, and I do not apologize for the questionable quality of some on the list. This type of association is not as satisfactory as recognition of the interval *per se* because

[66]

the effect of an interval depends upon its location in the scale. If such a list could be made up of intervals always beginning with the tonic, it might be more useful; but well-known melodies beginning with the tonic are difficult to find for some intervals. Since recognition of the effect varies if the direction is changed, the following lists may be of interest:

Up	*Down*
Half Step:	
Barcarolle, *Tales of Hoffman;* "Darling, I am growing older"	"Joy to the world"
Whole Step:	
"Silent Night"	"Believe me if all those endearing"; "Three blind mice"
Minor Third:	
Brahms' Lullaby	"Star-Spangled Banner"
Major Third:	
"Old Black Joe"	"Good night, ladies"; "Swing low, sweet chariot"
Perfect Fourth:	
Wedding March (*Tannhäuser*)	Soldier's Chorus (*Faust*); "Come, all ye faithful"

Perfect Fifth:

"Twinkle, twinkle little star"   "Bring a torch, Jeannette"

Minor Sixth:

"When Israel was in Egypt's land" ("Go down, Moses")   "O Zion, haste"

Major Sixth:

"My bonnie lies over the ocean"   "Over there";
"Nobody knows the trouble I see"

Minor seventh:

"Last night the nightingale"   "None but the lonely heart" (Tschaikowsky)

Major seventh:

Final duet in *Aïda*

Perfect Octave:

Elegie, Massenet   "Wait for the wagon"

Using known melodies to establish certain intervals may be a helpful device, but the best ear-training exercises are those which the student himself writes and performs as suggested in the preceding chapter.

Whenever Roman numerals are to represent harmonies, the teacher should insist upon a different symbol for a different sound. This will serve to remind the student of the sound under consideration.

Training the Ear

The abbreviations and symbols used in this book are as follows: for major triads (M.) large Roman numerals I, IV, V; for minor (m.) small Roman numerals ii, iii, vi; for diminished (d.) a small numeral with a zero exponent vii° and for augmented (A.) large numeral with a plus sign as exponent III⁺.

The use of hand-symbols for replies in ear-training is an excellent idea. In this way you can get a response from each member of the class independently, provided the eyes are kept shut. For instance, the use of an open hand for major, a fist for minor, a circle formed by the first finger and the thumb for diminished and the first and second fingers crossed for augmented triads gives you four symbols produced by one hand. These can be combined with fingers on the other hand for intervals up to five. All the triads of the key can be reported by using the fingers of both hands. If it is understood that the left hand represents the bass and the right hand the soprano position of the notes of a single chord, one, three or five fingers on each hand will take care of soprano and bass in root positions as well as inversions of triads. If the fist is used, this time not for "minor" but for the dissonant seventh, the chord members of the dominant seventh and other types of seventh can be indicated both in bass and in soprano. Closing the eyes improves student concentration and affords the chance to question all students at the same time. The blind hear so well because they have had to develop one sense to take the place of two. If the hand symbols are changed to represent more and more complex harmonies, they may be used for the five kinds of sevenths or chromatic pre-cadence effects, etc. With the sevenths it is a good idea to keep the logical historical order so that it will not be difficult for the student to remember the symbols. The historical order is also the usual text-book order: dominant seventh, half-diminished seventh (on the leading-tone in Major and the supertonic in minor), diminished seventh, minor seventh and major seventh, which one to five fingers may represent.

Much singing at sight should be continued as the ear is trained. I have no desire to add to the discussion of the value of syllables and of fixed-*do* versus moveable-*do* in sight-singing. The use of fixed-*do* is supposed to aid the development of absolute pitch, but letter names do that as efficiently and avoid the confusion resulting in this country from having two *sol-fa* names for the same pitch. The teacher should be able to use both fixed and moveable *do* as well as numbers of the scale and letters. He should also be able to sing syllables in minor starting from either *la* or *do* as tonic, although *la* is most used in this country. The use of letter-names corresponds in purpose to the use of fixed-*do,* and the use of numbers is a substitute for the moveable-*do* system.

For rhythmic ear-training several systems of spoken symbols have been formulated by Melville Smith and Max Krone, McHose and Tibbs (Eastman) and Bigelow *et al.* (at Northwestern). The Smith and Krone method accompanies the spoken symbols with written symbols which can be placed on the blackboard in rhythm so that the sound of a class using these symbols will be like that of a percussion section in an orchestra. The reader is referred to their texts, listed in the bibliography, for details.

There are various ways to combine keyboard training and ear training. Written orders may be prepared for a succession of students at the keyboard — for instance, directions to modulate from certain keys to definite related keys. The rest of the class is then given the initial keys and must report the end key of each modulation. Detailed suggestions for ear-training in modulation and more advanced work will be given in a later chapter. To the pessimistic declaration that little can be done about the musical ear, the teacher should affirm and believe that much may be accomplished.

CHAPTER V

Primary Triads in the Simplest Style

As you may have noted, the suggestions for assignments to students have not been in the form of exercises in which the teacher or author of the text may express his ideas but in which the student has little opportunity for self-expression. Rather, a student has been given an area in which he may play about as he pleases with materials which are familiar. To be sure, each area has certain limitations, and as soon as the student has made good use of his freedom in that field the fences should be removed and the area enlarged. Often the student will be the first to knock down fences or jump over them. (This is essentially the method used by Rimsky-Korsakoff

Primary Triads in the Simplest Style

in his harmony text although the English edition has obscured that fact by the addition of exercises of the usual type.) In Chapter I the rhythmic field was discussed; in Chapter II melody was added within the arpeggio or bugle-call, the scale, and combinations of both, all restrictions ultimately being removed. A suggestion of harmonic accompaniment came with the introduction of an open perfect fifth under the melodies. In this chapter the teaching of part-writing will be approached in the simplest style with the use of the primary triads.

Rhythms seem to ask for a change of pitch in melody. If we beat out a rhythm, its very accents seem to suggest higher pitches. Melodies in turn ask for changes of harmony. The perfect fifth as a bagpipe drone suggests two harmonies. The melodic tendencies of appoggiaturas to a triad suggest the alternating harmonies of the harmonica.

An order of importance both of the individual notes of the scale and of the triads built upon these notes will be found useful for many purposes (we shall see later that this order is also that of probability in doubling of notes in inversions as well as the order of choices for the next harmony). However, there are two kinds of importance in music as in the world in general: the importance or weight of position and that of activity or potential energy. The tonic triad represents the first and the dominant triad the second. (Root position also represents a position of authority; the inversions are more active, as we shall see later.) Since most of a composition, except possibly the last chord, is concerned with activity we will use the following as the order of importance for our purposes:

5	1	4	2	6	3	7
V	I	IV	ii	vi	iii	vii°

The first three of these are called primary triads and we may think of them as primary colors. (It is possible to classify all other combinations as modifications of these three chords much as all other colors may be derived from the three primary colors; Chaluez de Vernevil in his *Genuphonic Grammar* did this in 1850, and the idea persists in the twentieth century, although some have maintained that compositions of the present are all "dominant-harmony" throughout.)

In the following chapter we will take up our First Conjugation, which is related to the above order. At the outset we may think of the first three triads as a triangle:

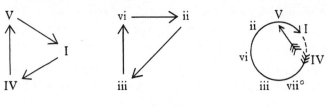

Primary Triads in the Simplest Style

(The secondary chords ii, iii and vi form another "triangle" for the primary triads of the minor mode, but that mode should be introduced in its own right where these triads become iv, v, i of minor.) For the combination of these six triads in the circle of the First Conjugation, see the diagram on page 109.

When we begin the primary triads in their simplest style we should emphasize not only their importance but their great beauty. Regardless of how elaborate the vocabulary becomes later, a student should not lose his affection for these most important words. The rhythms of Chapter II may be illustrated by striking the blackboard with the end of the chalk, beating out the design in a straight line. Melodies in Chapter III are two-dimensional for they can be graphed in contours, and even the sky-line of New York City and the mountains of South America have suggested melodies to composers. Harmony, which we are considering in this chapter, is at least three-dimensional and its simplest chords demand three notes. (When only two notes appear they may suggest harmonies but they are more like the meeting of two contours contrapuntally.) Triads then are like cubes or similar constructs. To be sure they may be sung melodically, as was suggested in the last chapter for ear-training:

(12)

Since aside from sounding the notes themselves, all discussion of them must be by similes, the reader may be interested in those found useful. In addition to the idea of colors the following analogies may be suggested: I is where we are, our home, the earth; IV is like the moon, placid, cool and remote; V, the powerful dominant, is like the sun. Or I is like the king; IV is the archbishop, the Amen-sayer, who agrees with the king in that he does not attempt to "change the king's mind" and disturb the tonal center. V is the prime minister, often more powerful than the king, changing at least temporarily the tonal center. It is said that the Chinese names for the notes of the scale contain references both to nature and to political government, so perhaps these analogies are not too fanciful. For the American youngster an analogy with the baseball diamond may help.

Primary Triads in the Simplest Style

I is of course the home-plate. IV is first base; V is third base from which the player wants to run "home." To complete the diamond shape we need a triad for second base; perhaps that is ii. When combined with ear-training based upon the student's holding either the tonal center or the leading-tone, these similes may help recognition.

After stipulating much creative experiment with a single triad, some texts deal with the dominant seventh and recommend composition and improvisation with the tonic triad and dominant seventh as background. Because of the element of dissonance and the problem of resolution it is simpler to take up the subject of voice-leading with the primary triads and that will be the order used here. These are usually taught in the four-voiced style of SATB writing. There is nothing very mysterious about voice-leading with triads if we use common sense and a little help from Mother Nature. I like to subdivide the problem under three headings:

I. How to write a chord

Nature in a sense writes the first triad for the physics laboratory to analyze. The fact that a sound possesses a series of overtones the lower notes of which form a major chord may be demonstrated at any piano in good tune; depress without sounding the keys of middle-c′ and e′ and g′ above it, explaining that this merely lifts the dampers from the strings. Then strike loudly the "Great C" (the first C below the bass clef); lift the finger of the left hand from the key and what you hear is the C major triad produced from overtones by sympathetic vibration. The arrangement of these overtones in nature dictates the answer to many problems of doubling and spacing in the simplest style:

(13)

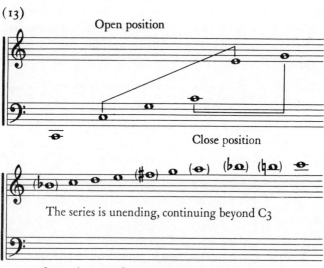

Open position

Close position

The series is unending, continuing beyond C3

[notes in parentheses are only approximate]

1. For four voices, double the roots (the overtone does).
2. Do not cross parts (it is common sense not to ask bass to sing higher than tenor, etc.).

Primary Triads in the Simplest Style

3. Both open and close position are good (both are found in the overtones). These are usually described as the three upper voices within an octave (close) or more than an octave from tenor to soprano (open); I have found it a good idea to stress the fact that root positions of triads in close position omit no notes in the vertical order of the three upper voices, but that in open position one note of the spelling is omitted between adjacent upper voices.

4. No gaps of more than an octave are found between soprano and alto or alto and tenor (none are found in the overtone system and if only one note is omitted in open position as above, no gaps will occur).

5. A gap of more than an octave may be used between bass and tenor (the strength of the lowest overtone of the bass fills this gap).

II. How to choose the next chord

1. It goes without saying that the melody note should be a member of the chord selected. With primary triads all but two of the notes of the scale have no options. The first and fifth have two possibilities.

2. When the notes of a soprano melody repeat, consider a possible change of the basic harmony. When the melody skips Mother Nature will aid the performer; if both notes are members

of the same overtone system, a single harmony will serve for both.

3. With a vocabulary of the primary triads I, IV, and V, there are always three situations possible: we may repeat the chord we have, or change to one of the other two. Dwelling upon one harmony for too long a time or changing harmonies all the time are extremes which we may well avoid. The rhythm of harmonic changes is an important feature of any style. There is no reason why a single harmony should not extend its influence over many measures. Actually, much depends upon the expectation which has been created. After we have been expecting one change in a measure, a sudden increase or decrease in the rate of change has to be justified or it may be awkward. Changes late in a measure are, as a rule, unexpected. As we have seen in an earlier chapter it is possible to accompany any melody, no matter how elaborate, with a single harmony; when a change occurs this often comes immediately following a barline. There is a reason for this. The first beat of a measure receives an accent; if I pull something new or different from my pocket, I at once produce an "accent" in the discussion since newness is a type of accent.

Primary Triads in the Simplest Style

Beginning with the melodic approach of Chapter III, the student may consider, after he has proved to his satisfaction that one accompanying harmony is sufficient, first where a dominant triad would be effective, adding that to his vocabulary or indicating it by a single note in a second voice to symbolize the triad. Surveys of the teaching of harmony have indicated that melodic decoration is left to the second year of theory in more than half of the colleges reporting! It is far better to start with elaborate original melodies and indicate possible use of the primary triads by single notes in a bass line than to postpone melodic decoration. Often the fewer notes in the second voice, the better, as more of the melody is recognized as possible decoration by the musical instinct of the student. When a larger vocabulary is introduced the order of importance given on page 74 is the order of probability as well.

III. How to lead the voices

1. The easiest way is usually best and it always remains effective and beautiful. (This is true in harmony as well as in performance; we speak of playing the piano, not of working the piano.) The easiest thing for a singer to do is to con-

tinue to sing the same note. Common sense suggests holding the note if it is also in the next chord. This is called a common tone, i.e., a tone held "in common" by two differing harmonies.

2. If the voice is to move, it is easier to move to the nearest available location in the next chord. This is also common sense; your coach of athletics would urge the shortest direction and not permit his men to jump the low hurdles as if they were high hurdles. The easiest way suggested in 1 above must be abandoned, however, if we are to harmonize a melody which rises by steps from the first to the sixth notes of the scale and returns. This represents a slight departure from the simple style now being discussed (a ballet dancer is different from a hurdler).

3. As long as you do not change your harmony you can do anything. Here there is no progression in a real sense, but merely changing dispositions, different chord tones in the soprano, or a change from open to close position and vice versa. Although stated as a matter of common sense at this beginning stage, the fact that the repetition of a harmony is not a progression proves useful throughout any advanced

stage of writing. (Remembering this would have saved many detailed rules concerning "hidden fifths," etc. in some texts.)

The "grammar" of music has certain similarities to the grammar of any language. As long as there is only one word (i.e·, one harmony) spoken or repeated, no error is possible. "Look! Look!" or any other command or interjection can be repeated for an hour and in any register of the voice without an error. In music, so long as the harmony is not changed no real error in grammar is possible; this statement may be extended to include inversions of a harmony as well as the same harmony at different registers or with different instrumentation. I would defend this statement even when presented with the following:

(14)

In my opinion we have here an unusual "orchestration" or choral effect of doubling in the tenor and soprano. It is not a grammatical error which contradicts the important generalization above. As a more radical illustration I would insist that no parallel fifths and no

effect of organum would be
heard in the following *tremolo*
because what is heard is only
the supertonic seventh of C
major.

(15)

4. So far, the overtone system and common sense
have sufficed to give us the principles upon
which the leading of voices
is based. There is one instance of historical preference yet to be discussed.
There is no question but
that the parallels in ex.
16 are easy to sing:

(16)

In fact, they were used without the thirds
before 900 A.D., and we are finding them
effective again in the twentieth century. This
parallel harmonization was called organum;
both that term and the later term fauxbourdon
are useful in the teaching of harmony. Since we
shall use these two terms repeatedly in later discussions, an explanation and a reference are
pertinent at this point. For a thorough treatment
of fauxbourdon the reader should consult an
historical survey by Ernest Trumble published
by the Institute of Mediaeval Music in Brook-
lyn. We use the term for a succession of two

or more first inversions of triads in which the roots are placed above the fifths, thus creating parallel fourths rather than parallel fifths. The upper voices are in parallel thirds and sixths with the lowest voice. Organum, in which parallel fifths and octaves occurred, was gradually superseded by fauxbourdon and the proscription of parallel fifths followed later. It is better to admit changes of historical preferences than to attempt to condemn parallel fifths and octaves on other grounds. Logically, perfect fifths in parallels are effective and they are increasingly used in the twentieth century. In fact, every time we play a melody in unisons there are parallel fifths sounding at the second upper partial, and organ registers are often used to reinforce them. During the period of common practice the "crudities" of the old organum were avoided. Most of the fifths in organum were a whole step apart; since chromatic parallel fifths do not remind the listener of organum, perfect fifths a half step apart have been used by many composers when the so-called German augmented sixth chord resolves to a triad. Many of the slip-chord effects of the twentieth century also involve chromatic parallel fifths.

(17)

Perhaps in keeping with the rise of. the individual in political history, the block-like parallel motion was gradually abandoned in favor of independence of voices, and what we know as contrary motion was introduced:

(18)

For three hundred years, roughly the period 1600 to 1900, musicians preferred this; accordingly, in IV to V or vice versa, if the bass ascends the three upper voices descend ; or the whole pattern is reversed: . No skip of a seventh or ninth between roots in the bass can be defended by common sense. These are adjacent degree progressions.

The student should now be encouraged to experiment within this simplest style and to improvise at

Primary Triads in the Simplest Style

the keyboard in both major and minor modes, then in a mixture of the two modes and in both harmonic and pure or modal minor. By using either major or minor triads on these primary degrees he can experiment with all the possible substitutes in minor: Dorian subdominant, the modal dominant, the Tierce de Picardie, etc., i.e., major or minor triads on each degree but the first: i-IV-I-v-i; i-iv-i-v-I; I-IV-i-v-i; etc. He may also experiment with the major-minor mode by starting with an initial major triad and using either major or minor triads on the other degrees. (There are many advantages in using a different symbol for a different sound as is done here. Such symbols are an additional emphasis upon ear-training, an emphasis lacking when all degrees are represented by large Roman numerals. At the keyboard the formula: I-IV-I-V-I is extremely useful.) Close position with three voices in the right hand is simplest. Different soprano positions produce

$$5 \overset{6}{\frown} 555 \; , \; \underset{7}{\underline{888}} \underset{}{\smile} 8 \; \text{ or } \; 3 \overset{4}{\frown} 3 \underset{2}{\smile} 3$$ as the melodic

figures. These patterns in the upper voice are easy to recognize, and even when the five chords are not played they serve as well as folk-tunes for identifying the first soprano note. Omission of the middle (tonic) chord results in the progression IV-V with correct voice-leading. When inversions are studied restore the middle chord to the formula but in its second or first inversion. The more ways in which a device can be used, the better!

A repetition of these five chords with a pause or breath after the first four produces a sentence with a half cadence and full cadence: I-IV-I-V, I-IV-I-V-I. This may be used to accompany many folk-tunes and well-known songs: "Way down upon the Swanee River," "Carry me back to old Virginia," "Annie Laurie," etc. A continuation V-I-V-I for contrast, followed by a return to the regular formula I-IV-I-V-I, will often take care of extended songs. If the student can harmonize for group singing, he should also be able to use these same successions for similar melodies notated on a third staff for vocal or instrumental solo.

It is impossible for the student to make mistakes of voice-leading within the limits of this simplest style. Instead of saying "Do not write parallel fifths or octaves," thus erecting signs of "Keep off the grass!", you show him the most natural paths. There has been no mention of overlaps or what might be called "geologic faulting of the strata" where the bass is higher than the tenor of the preceding chord, etc., because these will not occur except in such situations as the following where there is no objection:

(19)

Primary Triads in the Simplest Style

After an understanding of these simplest connections has been established, an alternative method of handling I-V-I or I-IV-I will make it possible to give greater range to soprano patterns. The use of the common-tone is given up so that the soprano may harmonize the first six notes of the scale; the same contrary motion diagrams used in IV-V-IV may be used and, since there is no objection to a change in the register of the bass, parallel motion in all four voices is also possible:

(20)

The so-called hidden fifths resulting may be ignored as they are found in the works of most composers.

After these simplest connections have been established it is a simple matter to extend these methods to cover all triads in what we shall call the three "conjugations."

[89]

CHAPTER VI

The Three Conjugations

IN some respects the teaching of harmony is similar to the teaching of a language. The scales are the alphabet, intervals are syllables and triads are words. With but one harmony it is as though we were able to say only: "See! See! See!" or rather: "Listen! Listen! Listen!" When we connect two triads they are almost like subject and predicate in relationship: "Birds fly" or "Dogs bark." Using such an analogy I would distinguish three different conjugations which may be considered regular conjugations or "regular verbs." Two of these regular conjugations are used in two ways each; that is, there are two ways of connecting triads somewhat similar to the idea of weak and strong verbs, although those words have connotations which make them inappropriate for our use here. The exceptions favored in certain progressions may be considered "irregular" verbs when the background of regularity has been established. As in a language, some progressions are irregular only in part and not in all voices.

The conventions of harmonic grammar which we are taking up in this chapter have historical validity. Music is not a "dead" language but one which is always changing. The period represented by these conjugations, roughly 1600 to 1900, gave one triad a central position as a goal of progression, setting up a system which we call tonality. Other methods of chord connection existed before and after this period and even to a certain extent during the period. The changes in styles occurred gradually and finally preferences confirmed by the taste of both composers and listeners found their way into the texts of theorists. If we can realize that the prohibitions of the typical grammar within what Piston calls the period of common practice are as they are because the earlier style of organum and even the strict use of modal flavor had disappeared, we will have a basis for understanding these prohibitions and for their acceptance or rejection today. It is also significant that illustrations of the overtone system in texts dealing with tonal harmony stop with the fifteenth or sixteenth partial, whereas the system is actually unending. Although the lower partials of the series seem to confirm tonality as the basic principle, the upper reaches contain very dissonant combinations and microtones enough for any modernist. This point alone may help students to realize at the outset that any text is based upon certain prejudices and presuppositions.

The First Conjugation

Basing these conjugations upon the supremacy of the tonic, reached through the cadence V-I (this cadence may derive from the second overtone, the first one different from the fundamental to which it tends to fall as to a ground), we set up a series of similar

relationships forming the circular diagram of our first conjugation:

If we substitute letters with C as the tonic we see why I recommended earlier that our circle of fifths

be written in the reverse of the usual order:

The Three Conjugations

A practical approach to most of the important procedures and generalizations is by way of the keyboard. With the roots in the left hand and with the derived spellings in three parts in the right hand it is not difficult even for the non-pianist to play the sequence of the first conjugation on the white notes

(21)   (a)

V - I - IV - vii° - iii - vi - ii - V - I

of the key of C major (ex. 21 a). These are the strongest progressions of all in the direction of the arrow, based upon the cadential principle. (The direction opposite to that indicated by the arrow will be discussed later. Between I and V and I and IV the double arrows indicate frequent movement in both directions.) Note that in the keyboard sequence both the common-tone-method and the contrary-motion-method are used because the latter occurs *between* the measures or steps of the sequence.

(b)

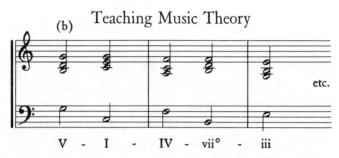

V - I - IV - vii° - iii

To make sure that these two methods of connection are heard and understood, have the players repeat each chord:

(22)

Parallel motion is also possible in all first-conjugation progressions since roots may move up or down a fourth or fifth in the bass as they please. It is better to state this at the outset than to begin by prohibiting parallel motion, a prohibition which can be seen in the first 99 pages of a well-known elementary text, and then say at that point that it is possible in all four voices when the roots are a fourth or fifth apart.

Keyboard sequences form a very efficient assignment, a much-in-little, for the more expert performers

The Three Conjugations

can be asked to play them in all keys. The triad vii°
is used in sequences so that this particular step of
the stairs may not be missing; however, it is omitted
in the list of ten progressions in each conjugation
when they are separately named later. For additional
variety in practice and in ear training other soprano
positions may be assigned (ex. 23-25):

(23)

(24)

(25)

Other doublings are, of course, possible; one is illustrated in ex. 26, which uses also the anti-arrow progressions to be discussed after the other two conjugations are introduced:

(26)

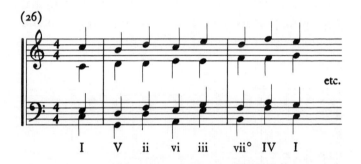

etc.

I   V   ii   vi   iii   vii° IV   I

The Second Conjugation

A possible source for the relationships in the second conjugation is found in the progression of a major to its relative minor. Three such situations are found in any major tonality: I-vi, IV-ii, and V-iii. The secondary triads have been often used as substitutes for the primary triads. In a sense they may be considered to be a master-servant relationship. At any rate, if a student confuses the direction of arrows used in this conjugation with the third one where the direction is reversed, a reminder that the most important progressions in this second conjugation have the relationship of major to relative minor helps.

[96]

The Three Conjugations

The complete conjugation is as follows:

I
vi
IV
ii
(vii°)
V
iii
I

The term "second" does not mean that progressions of this class are necessarily inferior to those of the first or superior to those of the third conjugation. The relative importance and the order of probability will be discussed later. The second conjugation really contains four kinds of relationship and the last two, last in conventional preference, reverse the order of the first two:

1. I-vi
   IV-ii
   V-iii

2. vi-IV
   iii-I

3. I-iii
   IV-vi

4. iii-V
   ii-IV
   vi-I

[97]

If we may consider the secondary triads as substitutes or servants in relation to the primary triads we might use the following analogies. The first three progressions in this second conjugation are like captains followed by privates in an army. If it is proper or expected that the captain enter the door before the private then the final three reversing this order are highly unusual. Continuing the analogy, section 2, vi-IV, might be likened to a lower rank in the army followed by a higher rank in the navy; at least vi and IV do not represent the same type of relationship as the progressions in section 1. The same consideration holds in iii-I.

We therefore find that I-iii and IV-vi are used fairly frequently, more than those in the last group. The frequent use of I-iii has been explained by Heinrich Schenker as *no* progression in the ordinary sense but as a change by "divider" from I to I⁶ with a passing note (the fifth of iii) substituted for the root I.

The Third Conjugation

Progressions in this conjugation are between chords on adjacent degrees. One of these, IV-V, has already been met in the chapter on primary triads. Common sense precludes the skip of a seventh or ninth be-

The Three Conjugations

tween roots. The most used direction in the last three hundred years has been *up* a step:

vi ↑
V
IV
iii
ii
I

The progressions of both the second and third conjugations may be practiced in their usual (arrow) direction in a single sequence. Thus, two keyboard sequences include all the possible progressions of triads in root-position in any tonality. They can be played in all keys and in the three positions for the soprano voice (ex. 27: a, b, c):

(27)   (a)

etc.

For the less usual progressions, play in reverse order.

Note that each *measure* forms the second conjugation in its more usual downward direction and that between measures progressions of the third conjugation are found in their usual upward direction. This fact may be emphasized by repeating each chord so that it may be heard as both the ending chord of one pair and the beginning chord of another progression:

(28)

I - vi vi - vii° vii° - V V - vi vi - IV

Now that we have introduced the diagrams of the three conjugations, their purpose and use will be discussed. If we could recapture the meaning of the word *progression* as musical terminology for the

The Three Conjugations

arrow direction and *regression* for the anti-arrow or reversed direction, we could make good use of that distinction. There is a sense in which the reverse order of the sequences just illustrated proves to be non-aggressive, less dynamic, more "other-worldly." It is more modal in effect and does not support the modern major-minor authority. Used exclusively, these reverse sequences sound pre-1600 or post-1900, "a la Palestrina" or like Debussy's revival of the modes. The arrows in the diagrams emphasize the fact that for every step in the direction opposite to that indicated by the arrows, there are many more in the direction of the arrows, a proportion at least nine to one. This statement is true not only of the music of the great composers of the period under discussion but of popular music and folk music, in fact, of any music in which tonality holds sway. The illustrations in F. J. Lehmann's *Harmonic Analysis,* drawn from many different sorts of composers, were certainly not selected to support any particular theory of directional movement such as we have outlined here, and yet in the first six illustrations only 6% of the progressions are in the anti-arrow direction. Or, consider any textbook of harmony giving exercises for realization. The same directions are found in any exercises based upon this period of common practice. To repeat this statement in terms that may interest a student who is now using a text in class: When the bass steps it steps *up*; when it skips a third it *descends*; and when it skips a fourth or fifth it moves in the direction of the tonic (see the figure for the first conjugation). In a textbook, basses given for chords in root position, or figured basses in any position, indicate an author's preferences in vocabulary and progression. Unfigured melodies in the same context are expected to be harmonized in the same general style, so it is wise to repeat at this point the suggestion that the student follow the arrows: up a fourth or down a fifth, down a third, and up a step. We shall do well to use these same progressions most of the time if we wish a natural or conventional setting of a melody in common-practice style. On the other hand, if we wish to write in a less conventional style it is a good idea to consider progressions in the opposite direction.

(29)

Schubert, *Piano Sonata in B-flat* (*Posthumous*), Fourth Movement, measures 86-91

The Three Conjugations

The first five brackets enclose anti-arrow movement in the second conjugation. The next three enclose anti-arrow movement in the first conjugation.

The three diagrams of the conjugations thus form the first important harmonic generalization. They retain their importance throughout the entire field of diatonic and chromatic harmony because the same pulls remain and the same progressions are favored no matter how complicated the structure raised upon their roots. We may add sevenths, ninths or elevenths to each, and alter the chords by the addition of many

[103]

chromatic accidentals, yet the same directions of harmonic pull are preferred.

These three classes constitute what might be likened
to the three "regular conjugations" of musically active
"verbs." Let us approach this same subject in a practical
way by considering all the progressions which are possible from each chord in any key (there are ten in each
conjugation when those involving vii° are omitted):

I   ii   iii   IV   V   vi   (vii°)   I   ii   iii   IV   V   vi   (vii°)   I

All possible combinations may be placed in one of
these three classes:

First Conjugation up & down 4 or 5	Second Conjugation up & down a 3rd (possible: a 6th)	Third Conjugation up or down a 2nd (Not a 7th)
I-IV	I-iii	I-ii
I-V	I-vi	ii-iii
ii-V	ii-IV	ii-I
ii-vi	iii-V	iii-IV
iii-vi	iii-I	iii-ii
IV-I	IV-vi	IV-V
V-I	IV-ii	IV-iii
V-ii	V-iii	V-vi
vi-ii	vi-I	V-IV
vi-iii	vi-IV	vi-V

As stated earlier, each one of the Roman numerals in
these lists represents a triad, and the kind of numeral

[104]

represents the kind of triad: large for major, small for minor, small with ° for diminished, and large with plus-sign for augmented (when that occurs in the minor mode). It is quite important that a different symbol be used for a different sound as an aid to ear training. These tables represent progressions in the major mode. The tables of numerals are the same for all possible progressions in the minor mode but the Roman numerals would be different since the harmonic minor scale, from which the conventional harmonies are derived, produces: i, ii°, III⁺, iv, V, VI, vii° as the types for these degrees. Each pair of numerals in these lists represents a progression of two triads. For instance: i-V in c minor represents a progression from c-e flat-g to g-b natural-d, and is in the first conjugation.

It is not necessary to memorize or refer to these tables in writing, since they can be readily remembered or reconstructed if we keep clearly in mind the way in which they are derived: they constitute *all* the progressions possible in root position within any one tonality and in either mode, for instance, C major or c minor. In these tables, which list each separate progression consisting of two chords only and not in sequence, the triad on the leading-tone vii° is omitted. Although that particular triad is used freely in sequences, it has not been much used in single progressions in root position, and therefore all progressions involving vii° are omitted in these tables. To reproduce these thirty progressions automatically, start from any one triad, for instance, I, and, calling it "one," count to the right or left, up or down the scale, four or five for the first-class progressions. Since up a fourth is the same as down a fifth and vice versa, counting in one direction up *or* down is quite sufficient; do the same from ii, etc. For the second class count a third and sixth, or simply think of the progressions of the second class as up or down a third. In fact, the skip of a sixth was considered a bit "inelegant" by some writers within the dates named (this has been indicated by enclosing the figure 6 above the column in parenthesis). Yet one does not hesitate to take a step which is a little less elegant or easy if the bass is in a location too high or too low for further progress, just as if a person were in a deep hole or on a high cliff. Skips of a sixth between roots in the bass are therefore found, but, other things being equal, a skip of a third is "handier" as the note is nearer at hand.

In the third conjugation the skip of a seventh between triads in root position was not much used in the common-practice period, and it is therefore easy to reproduce the third list by joining each triad with the one at its right and its left, on adjacent degrees above and below. Note that, in the thirty

The Three Conjugations

progressions listed, every triad with the exception of vii° has been connected with every other triad; for instance, I goes to ii in the third class, to iii in the second, to IV and V in the first class, and to vi in the second class.

There are ten in each class, and all progressions in the same class are alike in problems of voice leading; thus, just as you might learn a regular verb in Latin or French, learn the regular way in which all ten of the first class progressions behave. They are all alike in that each pair has one note in common; i.e., if you name the notes of I in some tonality (c-e-g), and of IV in the same tonality (f-a-c), there is one letter or note repeated. Similarly, in the second class each progression has two common-tones; but in progressions of the third class there are no common-tones and the historical preference has been for the use of contrary motion.

Contrary motion may also be used as an alternate method in the second conjugation:

(30)

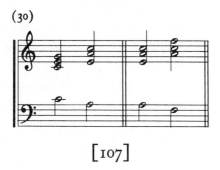

Another way to avoid the use of parallel octaves and fifths is to suggest that the soprano chord-position should change when the chord changes; i.e., changing chords should choose different members of the chords for melody. This is always true in the case of the fifth or octave in the soprano; it is possible, on the other hand, to have thirds of two successive harmonies in the soprano.

Many texts give tables indicating the order of probability for choices to follow the tonic chord; then, to follow the supertonic, etc. It is not necessary to consult such tables if the three conjugations are kept in mind. In fact, if you make such a table using the conjugations in order, you will reproduce for the most part these orders of probability. However, it is well to remember that third-conjugation progressions involving primary triads and a few other progressions may shift position in this ordering. Let us see what happens:

> Here we have mechanically followed each triad by the arrow and then the (anti-arrow) progression in each conjugation. This will serve in general as the order of probable choices, with a few exceptions: primary triads move forward; the deceptive cadence V-VI and certain other third conjugations are used with considerable frequency.

The Three Conjugations

	1st	2d	3d
I →	IV (V)	vi (iii)	ii
ii →	V (vi)	IV	iii (I)
iii →	vi	I (V)	IV (ii)
IV →	(I)	ii (vi)	V (iii)
V →	I (ii)	iii	vi (IV)
vi →	ii (iii)	IV (I)	V

It should be emphasized that the primary triads form a smaller circle within the first conjugation and that there are what might be called "shuttle-trains" between V and I as well as between I and IV in *both* directions. There is no such "shuttle-train" between IV and V as most of the traffic is in the upward direction. There is a similar smaller circle between the secondary triads but it is less used (iii, vi, ii of major being the equivalent of ii, v, i in pure minor):

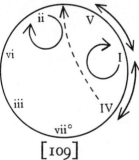

[109]

Teaching Music Theory

We have now summarized without recourse to prohibitions the progressions for all triads in root position. More extended sentences are in reality chains of progressions so that it should not prove difficult to write with at least "correct grammar" a statement of triads in root position in the major mode, for there are no exceptions or "irregular verbs" which are absolutely necessary in major. If most of the progressions are chosen in the direction of the arrows, including the two important "shuttle-trains," the results will not only be correct grammatically but will also agree with the logical sense of direction, forming musical statements similar to those in harmony texts and in music itself. Then, if you assign the composition of sentences exclusively from the anti-arrow progressions, the contrast in effect is obvious.

(31)

The usual arrow-directions

The Three Conjugations

Anti-arrow directions (modal and modern)

Movement in the less "hackneyed" direction is more original and often very effective:

(32)

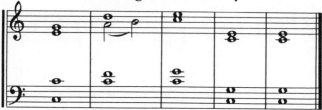

It was frequently used in the period before the victory of the major mode:

(33)

Palestrina, *Stabat Mater*

Downward steps in the third conjugation all contradict the expectations of modern tonality: either they sound like modal progressions with low leading-tones, or, when IV is followed by iii, the effect is that of the Lydian mode:

(34)

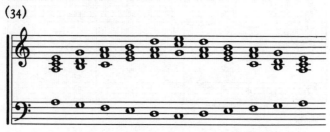

vi - V - IV - iii - ii - I - ii - iii - IV - V - vi

The Three Conjugations

In spite of the fact that all this line is in C major, the triad a-c-e, since it is also the tonic of a minor, seems to ask for G♯ in the next chord; and when we get a g-natural, this suggests a modal lowered leading-tone. On the contrary, a G-b-d triad followed by an a-c-e triad, as given in the usual direction at the end of the line, suggests no such contradiction since both chords are well-known in C major as a deceptive cadence. The effects in illustration 34 reappear in much modern music which has a modal flavor:

(35)

Debussy, *Pelleas and Melisande* (Act II)
(32 meas. before end of scene 1)

Permission for reprint granted by Durand et Cie., Paris, France, copyright owners: Elkan-Vogel Co., Inc., Philadelphia, Pa., agents.

If we try to discover the reason for the special flavor of the anti-arrow progressions in the other conjugations, we might reason as follows: in the second conjugation take ii-IV; ii, d-f-a, implies a seventh, c', and thus when f-a-c' follows, the root (d) no longer sounds, but little has been added to what was already implied. In the first conjugation, take ii-I; the d-f-a of ii implies the c' which wants to resolve to the third of V instead of passively taking its place in vi (a-c-e).

It is much better teaching to say that all thirty progressons are useful but that the unusual directions are "modal" than to say "Do not use IV after V." In art the word "never" should be avoided since there is a possible use for all available material. Regressions are not weak but less active, i.e., passive; they do not support the dominance of the tonic and, in fact, their use in impressionism pointed toward the downfall of autocratic tonality.

At this point we may close the first division of the subject. "Just a moment," protest some readers, "what about these rules: 'always use contrary motion in ii to V' and 'double the third of vi in V-vi, as usually stated?'" Those who raise these questions deserve an answer. There are *no* restrictions in the basic progressions discussed above for the major mode, provided there is no objection to a little modal flavor. Let us take the well-known progression already mentioned as a typical exception:

(36)

[114]

The Three Conjugations

Several different reasons have been given in harmony texts for an objection to holding the common-tone and moving to the nearest locations as in ex. 37. The reader can investigate the reasons stated by various authorities for preferring contrary motion.

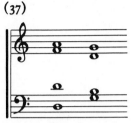

(37)

The ones most often expressed are the objection to the hidden octaves between alto and bass and the appearance of the tritone or augmented fourth in cross relation between f' of the alto and b' of the soprano in ex. 36. It is not surprising that you will find a wide variety of opinions expressed concerning this progression, differing also for various soprano positions. What is the real reason for this situation? In my opinion it is based upon the unsympathetic attitude of conventional harmony toward the modes. The real objection then is not the hidden octaves or the tritone but the lowered-seventh effect (f to g in the alto) and the Dorian-sixth effect of b-natural in the soprano following a minor chord of d, suggesting the Dorian mode:

(38)   "Dorian Sixth"

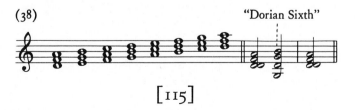

For those who like modal flavor, both of these effects are excellent; we may then expect to find a shifting attitude regarding this progression. Something similar may be said concerning the preference of the nineteenth century for (a) over (b) in the following:

(39)

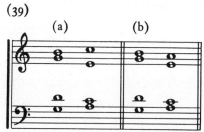

There is nothing incorrect about the second (b). It simply gives a more modal feeling, sounding more like the Aeolian mode or natural minor, rather than "C-majorish." To repeat: there are no exceptions absolutely necessary in the major mode among progressions in their three classes, but if you wish to emphasize a conventional major-feeling you will do well to take the leading tone to a doubled tonic in V-vi and to use contrary motion, the alternative method for first-class progressions, in ii to V. To teach and believe, however, that this must always be done is to disregard the changes that are occurring in a living language.

Sometimes students are taught to double the thirds of minor triads. A better statement is this: if you

The Three Conjugations

want to reinforce the dominance of *primary* tonal centers, double the thirds of *secondary* triads for you will then be doubling primary notes of the key. This statement covers the ii°, III⁺, and VI (diminished, augmented and major triads) found in the minor mode as well as the secondary triads in major, all of which happen to be minor triads. The problem of "irregular verbs" or exceptions in the minor mode will be considered in the next chapter, where we shall meet these same progressions again.

We have seen that a progression in the arrow-direction is active rather than passive in effect. If the second chord of an anti-arrow progression is inverted, *it* becomes more active and the progression is in a sense, modernized. This is true of all fifteen regressive connections. The effect of inversion upon a harmony will be considered at some length in Chapter VIII. Here a comparison of the following will serve as proof of the above statement:

(40)

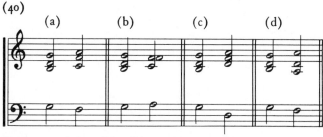

Compare (a) with (b) and (c) with (d).

Inverting the second chord energizes it and turns what might be called a regression into a progression. As we shall see in Chapter VIII, inversions are dynamically active. However, it cannot be too strongly emphasized that if you wish to write in a less conventional and more modern style you should use more root-progressions in the direction opposite to the usual one. They are very beautiful, as the Schubert and Debussy illustrations witness; they are "democratic" as they do not set the "king" so securely on the throne; they are "other-wordly," modal, religious, "prayerful," non-aggressive and yet very effective in their way.

CHAPTER VII

Generalizations in the Minor Mode

WITH the purpose of clarifying harmonic procedures, three conjugations have been presented in
their simplest connections for the leading of the voices.
No exceptions were found necessary in the major mode
and all progressions may be handled in the regular
methods used for the three conjugations, provided we do
not object to a little modal flavor. However, there are
six exceptions, or what we may call six "irregular
verbs," among the thirty progressions in the minor
mode. With respect to these it is not merely a question of admitting modal effects which, though austere,
are a part of our European background. The prob-

lem involves an "oriental" augmented second, which occurs in the following six progressions when the "regular" treatment of the preceding chapter is used.

(41)

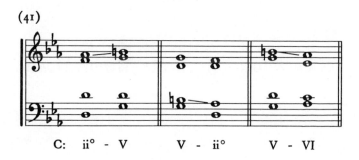

It would be as unwise to ignore the desire of Western musicians to avoid these in harmonic progression as it would be to deny the melodic beauty and effectiveness of the augmented second when used as a figuration of some harmonic galaxy or for coloristic effects:

Generalizations in the Minor Mode

(42)

Rimsky-Korsakoff, *Le coq d'or*, Act II, measure 502-3*

Ah ——— les — fleurs ——— sont —

tôt ——— fa - né - - es ———

We should retain the generalizations of the three conjugations, each containing ten pairs of triads, and then relate the exceptional treatment, used to avoid these augmented seconds, to the generalizations. Harmony texts usually give explicit instructions for at least two of the six but students still have difficulty in handling them without references to the foundation of regularity already established. The progressions ii°-V and V-ii° belong in the first conjugation. The alternative method which abandons the common-tone and uses contrary motion or even parallel motion is the sole method used in the minor mode:

*Used with permission of the original publisher: Robert Forberg, Bad Godesberg, Germany.

[121]

(43)

The progressions V-VI and VI-V belong to the third conjugation. Remembering this classification is still important here because these two progressions become exceptions in the minor mode only for *one* voice, thus are still within that conjugation. It may be a good plan to think or write the progression as though it were *no* exception and then to correct the skip of the augmented second by taking the leading-tone up to a doubled tonic:

(44)

It is true that the result is a doubled third of VI with two voices moving up and two down, but merely to start with any such mechanical instruction as "double the third of VI" without giving the background of regularity and the reference to the third conjugation upon which to base the slight irregularity, can lead to the most astonishing errors in which the

Generalizations in the Minor Mode

instruction is followed and yet we are without good voice-leading.

The other two exceptions, III⁺-iv and iv-III⁺ are relatively so unimportant that they are usually ignored by harmony texts or given scant attention. It is true that they are seldom used, but if we are to have a thorough and complete account of harmonic progressions they must be included. Here we are faced with a choice of "evils": parallel fifths, one of them augmented, *or* the appearance of the augmented second. Western music seems more ready to re-admit parallels, which are not entirely foreign to a European habitat, than to admit augmented seconds. In these progressions write the hidden fifths in parallel motion, one of them augmented and one perfect, and then avoid the augmented second by doubling the third of III⁺ (45a) or the fifth of iv (45b):

(45)

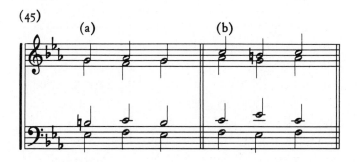

You may decide that these progressions are too dissonant for your purpose and therefore scarcely worth consideration; they should nevertheless be included in any complete list of progressions, just as we expect to find every irregular verb listed in a French grammar. These last two illustrations have been given in a condensed arrangement of three chords to emphasize the generalization that, so far as voice-leading is concerned, if a road is good to take in one direction, the way is also good in the reverse direction. The end result, the degrees of activity of the two chords, may be different — and possibly in these days of one-way traffic the simile of the road is not entirely appropriate! It does, however, point to the fact that although there are six exceptions in the thirty progressions in minor, two in the first conjugation and four in the third, they are really two times three exceptions, of which the last pair is seldom used.

Returning to the two pairs of exceptions which are most important in the minor mode: ii°-V-ii° and V-VI-V, we discover that they are the same exceptions which we discussed in the major mode, where many conservative theorists insist upon contrary motion in the first and a doubled third of VI in the second, handling them the same in both modes. It would look as if there were here an opportunity to

Generalizations in the Minor Mode

make a single generalization covering their treatment in both major and minor, thus saving time and effort on the part of both teacher and student. It is not advisable to do so because we would not have a completely correct statement; it would not represent the present state of the language as far as the major mode is concerned. In addition there is an advantage in using as a foundation, techniques which are completely regular in the major mode, provided the question of irregularities is faced as it arises.

One effective suggestion to give your students in connection with the irregular verbs found in the minor mode is this: approach (and leave) the leading-tone (the note with the accidental) from *above*. This refers to the fact that diminished intervals are easier to sing than augmented ones. All the notes above the leading-tone form good melodic intervals:

(46)

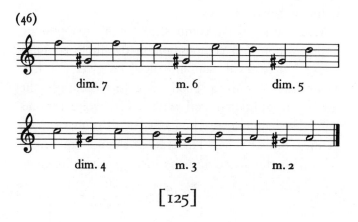

but only two of the six from below are easy melodic approaches:

(47)

The skips of the major third and sixth are easy because they are in fact members of the same dominant triad. Accordingly, they are fine when the harmony remains dominant but are not so likely to occur in changing harmonies. The major seventh is a strong interval, though less conventional, employed in the twentieth century.

Much can be accomplished with root-position improvisation and composition in the three conjugations. No basses or sopranos need be given for harmonization. It is a good idea to encourage the use of an additional staff with a fifth voice for melodic decoration, as was suggested with primary triads in the simplest style. The student should experiment with both the active and the more passive directions,

Generalizations in the Minor Mode

i.e., with progressions in the direction of the arrows combined with the "shuttle-trains" between triads and the regressive connections (anti-arrow direction). However, there is a static quality about the persistent use of root positions, and the use of inversions should not long be delayed.

The idea that a cadential six-four is a decorated dominant helps the student to avoid the parallels which might result from IV to I_4^6:

(48)

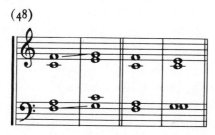

This is really a progression of the third conjugation (IV-V) in which the regular procedure is to approach the doubled root of V (the doubled fifth of I) by contrary motion, as in all third-class progressions

The preference for fauxbour-bon over organum is also useful in the approach to I_4^6 from the supertonic:

(49)

(50)

The student will be quick to see and hear these different effects; and referring this also to an historical preference is better than a definite command: "In ii or ii⁶ to V, place the roots above the fifths."

One final caution is necessary in all references to the use of the three conjugations as regular technical processes: it is necessary that both chords under consideration be in the same key before they can be so referred. The chord of C major followed by the chord of D major for purposes of reference is I-ii (third raised) in C, or IV-V in G, etc., and not a first conjugation I in C to V in G. With this caution in mind we will find the conjugations useful in the chapters on seventh chords, chromatic harmony and modulation.

If the objection is raised that "all generalizations are faulty," we should reply that a logician will immediately add: "all generalizations are faulty, including this one: 'all generalizations are faulty.'" I believe that some are possible in this field. As in a bird's-eye view, generalizations indicate the main highways so that the student will not become lost in his exploration of those by-ways which interest him as he develops his individual style. There are two kinds of strength in the world as in music, one of solidity or stolidity, possessed by root position, and the other the strength of potential movement, which the inversions possess. Any example shows this:

(51)

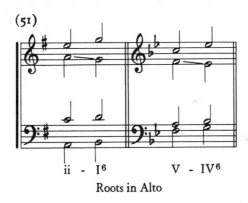

ii - I⁶   V - IV⁶

Roots in Alto

Contrary motion to the successive roots rather than to successive bass notes is a good suggestion for early work with inversions, but the possibilities when inversions are used are too varied for generalizations. In a way we have repeated here something akin to the relative differences between the triads themselves, dis-

cussed earlier. To say that inversions are weaker (as
Wedge does) is to ignore the fresh kinetic energy
they introduce. Try connecting every major and
minor triad with every other such chord and you
will realize that by no means all the possibilities for
connecting triads have yet become exhausted.

(52)

More will be said about these possibilities in connection with the problems of theory in the twentieth
century.

CHAPTER VIII

The Effect of Inversions

I NVERTING a triad increases its activity or dynamic potential. If we illustrate a triad in root position as a pyramid on its base: △ , we may say that the first inversion is this pyramid on its apex: ▽ . There is less specific gravity in first inversions. They are less stable and, like stepping-stones in a brook, they are most useful when near solid ground on each side, in other words, connected with triads in root position by a step in the bass. Large skips between two first inversions need about the same care that large jumps between the stepping-stones of our illustration demand; usually the chord before or after the first inversion is in root position. There are no generalizations for voice-leading that will insure correct connections and automatically avoid all errors as in the conjugations for root-position, but the following sequence of the first conjugation would be a good introduction at the keyboard:

(53)

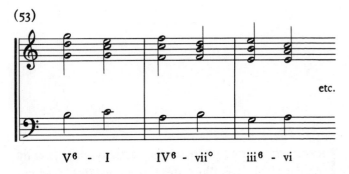

etc.

V⁶ - I   IV⁶ - vii°   iii⁶ - vi

First Conjugation

We used in the discussion of root-positions the historical terms organum and fauxbourdon; in the introduction of inversions I find the latter term very useful. This historical preference has persisted and you may call attention to its presence in three voices of the series:

[132]

(54)

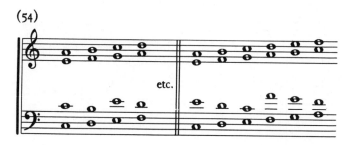

etc.

The fourth voice in order to avoid duplicating one
of the three voices of the fauxbourdon, doubles in
alternate fashion the various chord members: root,
third or fifth. Calling attention to the fauxbourdon
is better than commanding "place the fifths above the
roots." Parallel fifths instead of parallel fourths are
effective as "bell-effects" (ex. 55) since the overtone
of the fifth is particularly prominent in bells; in
the lower register of the voices it suggests a feature
of organum which harmony texts were careful to
avoid. There is an alternative, non-sequential method
for the third-conjugation series of first inversions. This
is the use of contrary motion in the three upper
voices, the usual method for that conjugation. The
doubling of the nearest notes in each case results in
a doubled third (bass) in each chord:

[133]

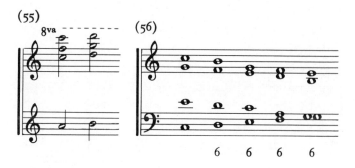

I cannot agree with those theorists who state that inversions are weaker than root positions. In fact, we may arrange an order of relative activity and say that it increases in the following series: root position of triads, first inversion of triads, second inversion of triads, root position of seventh chords, first inversion, second inversion and third inversion of seventh chords, the last inversion being the most volatile. Of course, the five kinds of diatonic sevenths differ in their degree of activity as well.

Because of the increased energy in the first inversion a very important generalization can now be emphasized: if we take every progression of the three conjugations in the unusual or inactive direction, i.e., the direction opposite to that of the arrows, and place the second chord in its first inversion, the progression *becomes* active and is one frequently found in

[134]

music of the last three centuries. If we use the expression "cart before the horse" for progressions in the "passive direction," inversion now has the effect of putting a motor in the cart and energizing the progression. All fifteen of the progressions in the less usual direction should be played with the second chord in its first inversion to demonstrate the truth of this generalization. Another keyboard sequence using these is effective: I-V^6-vi-iii^6-IV-I^6-ii-vi^6, etc. A sequence involving the second conjugation: I-vi^6-vii-V-vi-IV^6, etc., in the usual direction is not as strong as the less usual direction with the second chord inverted; the repeated bass of the above is now changed to a skip of a fourth: vi-I^6-V-vii^6-IV-vi^6, etc.

If we may consider the first inversion a pyramid upon its apex, the second inversion is a pyramid in the process of falling: ▽ . In musical terms the second inversion is a cadential effect, the word cadence meaning "to fall." It is true that one may "float" on a series of second inversions as if on a succession of clouds:

(57)

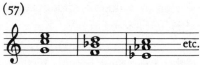

without touching the ground in between — but all the time we know that we are merely defying the law of gravity and postponing the natural result which would bring us down to earth (César Franck in his third Organ Chorale and the Symphony in d minor, measures 57-58, used this effect; the triumphant uses of this inversion for successive climaxes by R. Strauss, avoiding the expected cadences after each, may be found in the opera *Salome,* beginning 94 measures from the end).

It is possible to divide the entire harmonic vocabulary, chromatic as well as diatonic, into three groups of chords: pre-cadence, cadence, and final, in which the most famous representatives appear (in the same order) as IV-V-I. In the pre-cadence classification we have chords which do not contain the leading-tone: IV, IV^6, ii^6, vi, I^6, etc., plus the chromatic effects of Chapter XI. In Chapter IX some secondary sevenths are added to this classification, the most important being ii^7, which is really IV plus ii; its first inversion is one of Bach's favorite pre-cadence chords. In the second group, the cadence chords, we should place the I$^6_4$ since it is a delayed dominant chord usually appearing as a double appoggiatura (iii^6, presenting all the connotations of V^{13}, is a single appoggiatured V in this same group). That I$^6_4$ has this effect is further supported by the fact that the ear's response to I$^6_4$ on the part of elementary students will often be "V." This interpretation explains why

The Effect of Inversions

the $^6_4$ effect is a cadencing effect, why we double the bass (fifth of uninverted triad) and why the only chord which can be used in its second inversion as a "real chord" is the tonic; if you jump to, or accent, any other $^6_4$ it becomes tonic, i.e., you have modulated:

(58)

$$\text{vi}\,^6_4 = \text{i}\,^6_4$$

a) cadence in a minor expected

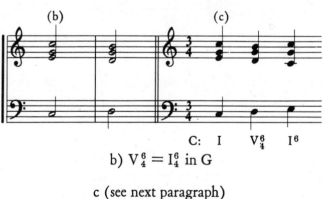

C: I   V$^6_4$ I^6

b) V$^6_4$ = I$^6_4$ in G

c (see next paragraph)

[137]

Other second inversions than that of the tonic can be used provided they are *not* chords in the strict meaning of chords as important supporting columns in the structure. If they can be explained as melodic decoration they may be said to vanish, and the statement that the second inversion of the tonic is the only one used still holds. It is true that some theorists go further and deny the existence of any second inversion as a true chord. Because of its prominent position in the cadence this does not seem a practical point of view. All the other uses outside the cadence can be associated with three illustrations or their combinations (approaching by one method of decoration

(59)

(a)

(b)

and leaving by another): The technical names associated with the illustration above are: (a) the auxiliary or embellishing $^6_4$, (b) the bass-figuration $^6_4$,

The Effect of Inversions

and (c) the passing $^6_4$. They are often described as

being *between:* (a) two chords having the same bass-note, (b) two different positions of the same harmony, and (c) adjacent bass-notes in a three-note row. The important word in this last sentence is "between." Associating them with well-known music helps in their recognition: (a) with "Silent Night" or the last two measures of the "Wedding March" from *Lohengrin,* (b) with "Onward Christian Soldiers" or the alternating tonic and dominant bass of almost any military march, (c) with the "Spanish Hymn"; or, since the chord on either side may be any harmony containing the adjacent note, merely with the game "tit-tat-toe, three in-a-row." In elementary work they are typically used between triads and their first inversions: two voices pass, one voice holds and the fourth voice is an auxiliary note in that situation; cf. (c) above, where the bass and alto voices pass in contrary motion as in "tit-tat-toe," the tenor repeats and the soprano is an embellishment. It is evident that no *chord* exists at this point. In more advanced writing the chords on either side of the passing second inversion may be anything in the musical vocabulary if the three-note row is kept in the bass (59d).

The best method for the recognition of each diatonic triad by ear is that which relates them to a tonal center (*do*) or its neighbor (*ti*). Melville Smith and Max Krone in their *Fundamental Musicianship* (Volumes I and II) use this method, emphasizing that the tonic major triad rises from *do* as root and the subdominant triad falls from the same tonic as fifth; the submediant triad, a minor chord, has *do* as third. The dominant triad, however, has the leading-tone as third and the minor triad on the mediant has the leading-tone as fifth; the diminished triad on vii of course has the leading-tone as root. The only triad not yet connected to this lifeline of tonic and leading-tone is the supertonic; however, it is possible to connect it with *do* as an added seventh. It is this feeling of a seventh understood which is probably the reason why ii is followed by V, since the implied seventh can then be resolved to the third of V.

[140]

Generalizations regarding
Seventh Chords

A NEW term appears for the first time in our discussion when another third is placed on top of the two thirds forming our consonant triads: the word "resolution." The seventh is a dissonant element. If we use the homely illustration of dirt suspended in water and "dissolve" for "resolve," we have a parallel to the usual behaviour of this element in the chord: it falls. When this occurs we have the following three possibilities in most frequent use:

(60)

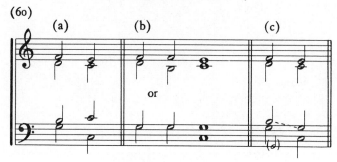

(a)   (b)   (c)

or

(♩)

(a) complete to incomplete
(b) incomplete to complete
(c) both complete by the tenor's
      sacrifice

(c) presents a sacrifice on the part of the leading-
tone to make a complete final tonic possible. Some
consider it among the "irregular resolutions" but
I find it more satisfactory to consider the behaviour
of the seventh as determining the regularity or irregularity of the progression. When we emphasize the
word sacrifice we may illustrate it in baseball or simply state that a sacrifice is the more real, the more
a person or a voice wishes to go in one direction but
goes in another for the good of the other voices and
the whole. The leading tone, as its name implies,
has a strong desire to ascend to tonic. However, the
sacrifice is seldom found in the soprano; the "prima
donna" does not sacrifice as a rule.

Generalizations Regarding Seventh Chords

These three regular resolutions are the same for all first-conjugation progressions in the cadencing direction (ii^7-V, vi^7-ii, etc.); no special rules are needed for progressions other than V^7-I. Where such special rules are spelled out it seems as if authors of texts in harmony are trying to make their books as long as possible. For facility at the keyboard using dominant sevenths, have the students play V^7-I, in five parts, through tonalities one half-step, and, following that, one whole-step apart. In the latter case each chord can be made a dominant seventh and then we have the famous cliché of a chain of dominants (cf. Chapter XI).

Irregular resolutions of seventh chords are so multitudinous that it is not necessary to dwell upon them in detail (when V^7 goes to I^6 there must be an irregular resolution because the bass has preempted the note of resolution: (61)

The same is true of a second conjugation in root position: (62)

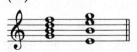

The anti-arrow or non-cadential direction in the first conjugation also does not resolve the seventh:

[143]

(63)

Substitutes for the completely authentic cadence are possible:

(64)

| half plagal and half authentic (vii°⁴₃) | three-fourths plagal and one-fourth authentic | one-fourth plagal and three-fourths authentic |

Musicians in the twentieth century believe that any dissonance may proceed to any other dissonance. However, let us emphasize first that five or more chapters on progressions involving diatonic sevenths are not necessary. They all behave in similar fashion; and the half-diminished seventh on the leading-tone of the major mode, the fully diminished seventh on the same position in the minor mode, as well as the secondary sevenths, can be covered in generalizations for the three conjugations. The following sequence, which is not difficult to play in the key of C major, illustrates the first conjugation in its usual direction:

[144]

Generalizations Regarding Seventh Chords

(65)

It is easier to introduce this sequence as above in five parts, particularly as it is then easily changed into a sequence involving continuous sevenths (b). To reduce the above to the smoothest four-part writing or playing omit the lowest voice of the treble clef (the thumb of the right hand). Note that in the continuous sevenths of (b), every other chord is incomplete when the sequence is reduced to four voices. From this same sequence we can introduce the use of inversions in the first conjugation. Return to the five parts but omit the left hand and you introduce the second inversion of every other seventh. Mechanically the two upper voices descend and then the two lower voices.

(66)

Beginning with a first inversion we secure, by lowering the inner and outer voices alternately, third inversions as well.

[145]

Taking the same dominant seventh on the upper staff the second conjugation can be played in its usual direction by lowering one voice at a time:

(67)

The resolution in the third conjugation is quite important. Although it appears in the deceptive cadence V^7 to vi, I prefer to introduce it on all degrees, beginning with vii°^{7}-I, as follows:

(68)

Singing these resolutions (ex. 69) stresses the fact that they contain the main tendencies for voice-leading in the diatonic scale.

(69)

Generalizations Regarding Seventh Chords

The leading-tone seventh of the major mode is taken to the tonic in three ways: (1) the third of the tonic is doubled and this is always satisfactory; (2) the root of the tonic may be doubled provided the three upper voices are in "fauxbourdon," or (3) the fifth may be doubled. The important generalization is that these same three resolutions serve for all types of sevenths. Merely prefix the above with the signature of two flats and you have I⁷ going to ii; the signature of three sharps gives you ii⁷ to iii, etc., until you reach the important deceptive cadence V⁷ to vi in E or E♭ major. The same demonstration can be played as a sequence on the piano in one tonality:

(70)

etc.

If we think of these sevenths as satellite or attendant chords to the following triad, we can anticipate the fact that all five of the usual sounds of seventh chords (dominant, half-diminished, diminished, minor or major sevenths) make good attendant chords with roots at both half-step and whole-step distances:

[147]

(71)

They are all possible attendant chords to any minor triad as well.

The efficiency of generalizations concerning part-writing may be demonstrated: although most texts on harmony discuss the diatonic progression of the deceptive cadence V^7-vi or V^7-VI, devoting another chapter to secondary sevenths I^7-ii, ii^7-iii, etc., with two more chapters given to the resolution of the leading-tone seventh in the major mode and of the diminished seventh to a minor tonic, these are all the same progression so far as the best methods of resolution and voice-leading are concerned.

[148]

Generalizations Regarding Seventh Chords

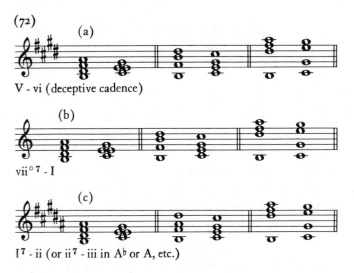

(72)

(a)

V - vi (deceptive cadence)

(b)

vii°⁷ - I

(c)

I⁷ - ii (or ii⁷ - iii in A♭ or A, etc.)

Note that these are all in "Third Conjugation"

Diminished sevenths in the minor mode are resolved
to the tonic in the same way. As we shall see in
the chapter on chromatic harmonies, this third conjugation is used with diminished sevenths as satellite
chords around every triad of the scale. The diminished seventh is a chameleon-like chord. There are
only three such sounds in all music and each diminished seventh has the notes of another diminished
seventh as possible progenitors in dominant minor
ninths:

[149]

(73)

The two ambiguous intervals (diminished fifths) make an ambiguous chord; we do not know its root. Changing one note (or three notes) by half-steps produces a dominant seventh (which may also explode as an augmented sixth to many keys, as described in Chapter XI). No wonder this sound is at home anywhere but may easily be abused if overworked. For diatonic sevenths in the minor mode the leading tone is lowered in III^7 and i^7 and raised only in the final cadence. For instance, this first-conjugation sequence sounds as if it were in the relative major, except at the cadence:

(74)

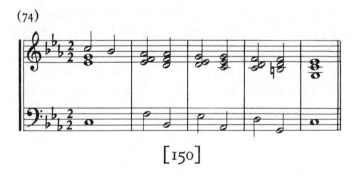

Generalizations Regarding Seventh Chords

This reduces the usual sounds of the seventh chords to five types: the dominant seventh, the half-diminished, the diminished, the minor and the major. The following is an interesting way to sing them in arpeggios, changing one note at a time:

(75) Singing:

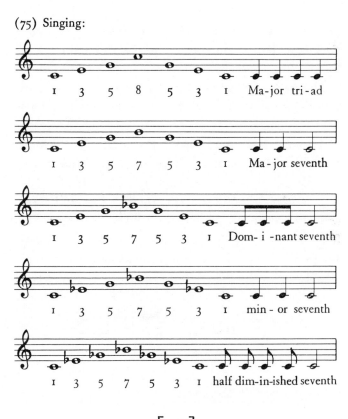

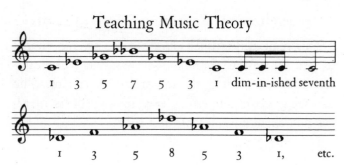

This should aid ear-training; have students try, with closed eyes but, we hope, open ears, identification by one to five fingers when the order is varied in dictation.

The order in which the harmonic vocabulary is introduced varies with different teachers and authors of texts. Some prefer to introduce the dominant seventh as the first new chord after a single tonic chord has been exploited. If it is introduced at this point, we can scarcely avoid discussing its usual resolutions. If it is introduced after the primary triads and their simplest treatment, remind the student that the addition of a seventh does not change the classification: IV to V^7 is still in the third conjugation; therefore all moving voices use contrary motion. There are two possibilities:

(76)

Generalizations Regarding Seventh Chords

If the seventh is held over ("prepared" is the usual terminology), all other voices continue to go to the nearest locations by contrary motion, and the result is an incomplete dominant seventh. However, all voices may descend, in which case the dominant seventh will be complete. Reminding the student of the conjugation helps to avoid errors frequently found.

The last inversion of chords of the seventh appears very simply as a passing-tone within the second conjugation:

(77)

Here we have held the three upper voices while the bass descends. Somewhat the reverse of this idea is the repetition or holding over of the bass-tone while the rest of the harmony uses a third conjugation in the usual direction:

(78)

Note the fauxbourdon arrangement of the upper voices.
Organum is less usual although it is reappearing in the
twentieth century: (a)

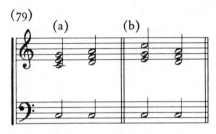

Contrary motion (b) is, of course, also satisfactory.

In the next chapter we will explain the indexing
of vocabulary. In indices, as in the keyboard sequences
in this chapter, the tonic seventh and the mediant
seventh of the harmonic minor mode have been omitted. These last two are sometimes named by both
the triad and the seventh: minor-major seventh and
augmented-major seventh; when, similarly, the minor
seventh is called the minor-minor seventh and the
major seventh, the major-major seventh by certain
texts based on German terminology, unnecessary waste
of breath results.

CHAPTER X

Indexing the Harmonic Vocabulary

IT is possible for students of harmony to learn to be at home in all tonalities, major and minor, and at the same time to secure a practical index of some of the many available harmonies, an index which will prove useful in composition or improvisation. Before explaining a partial index in detail, we may state that it is based upon the plurisignificance of any one note in many chords and the appearance of the same note in many scales. This word "plurisignificance," used by Bernard Ziehn in important theoretical works now out of print, will be shortened to "index" here, in order to suggest uses to which this method for organizing a vocabulary systematically may be adapted.

Teaching Music Theory

Performing an index — at the piano, or better still, singing an index in arpeggios or figurations without aid from a piano — is as accurate a measure of general musicianship as any one test can afford. The person who performs or writes an index correctly, stating all the locations at which its chords are found, in the shortest time, has the best facility and most thorough acquaintance with all tonalities. However, to further encourage the study of indices, the following important generalization is given at once:

Any two harmonies (or all harmonies) of any one index are effective in succession, in any order. In more elaborate chromatic harmony, any chords from adjacent indices are also possible in succession.

If one has a thorough acquaintance with tonalities, scales and signatures, he may begin to practice and use an index without any other instruction in harmony. Triads are "born" on each degree of the two scales used: the major and the harmonic minor. These triads are called "diatonic," i.e., derived from the diatonic scale. By comparing their sounds we find that there are only four kinds, which we may diagram so as to show the twelve locations of the note we shall index. Let the box ☐ equal a major third and a smaller box ☐ represent a minor third. The structure of a major triad places the smaller box on top of the larger and the total, or a box which includes both, is called a perfect fifth. The minor triad reverses the two boxes without changing the size of the composite box. Diminished triads contain two small thirds and consequently the containing box is a diminished fifth. Augmented triads contain two large boxes and the total is an augmented fifth. Major and minor triads take their name from the lower interval, diminished and augmented intervals from the intervals of the combined sizes or fifths:

	M	m	d	A
	3 m.3 -6	M.3	9 m.3	12 M.3 11
Perf. 5	2 M.3 5	m.3 -4	8 m.3 -7	M.3 -10

This information is reviewed here because the problem of indexing triads, in its simplest terms, is to locate a given note at all twelve points; it may be placed as the root, third or fifth of four different types.

The result for c^2 is:

(80)

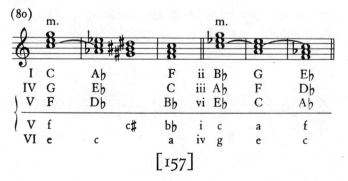

	m.				m.		
I	C	A♭		F	ii B♭	G	E♭
IV	G	E♭		C	iii A♭	F	D♭
V	F	D♭		B♭	vi E♭	C	A♭
V	f		c♯	b♭	i c	a	f
VI	e	c		a	iv g	e	c

Since there are only twelve different notes within the octave, there are only twelve different indices to practice in terms of the keyboard. However, music uses enharmonic spellings and this adds to the possibilities in writing. All the usual spellings may be included in the twelve indices, provided that whenever a triad is well-known in two spellings it is written enharmonically, with all three chord members changed, and located in both tonalities. In some cases, one spelling is better known in one location and another in another location. For useful practice in spelling and thinking enharmonically it is advisable to limit the keys used in the indices to tonalities containing not more than six accidentals, The student should sing indices in arpeggio fashion:

(81)

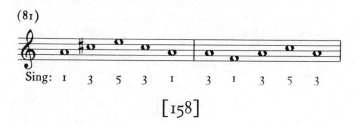

Sing: 1 3 5 3 1 3 1 3 5 3

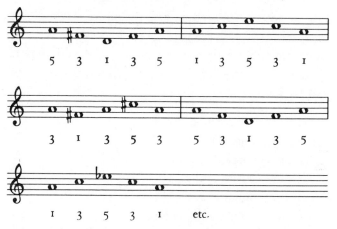

By the use of sequences drawn from the conjugations the student can also prove that the indexed chords are diatonic in the fifty-two tonalities listed for the twelve chords.

Instead of adding the locations to an index already constructed from the intervals or "boxes" in the triads, it is possible, if the lowest note is given or has been correctly determined for each triad, to use the locations of these lowest notes for the spelling of the triads. The result is the same and the line of thought may be of even greater value since, when a tonality enters a musician's mind, all the triads of that tonality will appear almost simultaneously as the family of triads of that key; for instance, in the sixth measure of the index of C we secure the lowest note as a perfect fifth below c^2; when this f′ is found it is located as ii of E♭ major, and the signature of three flats adds the flat to the middle note a′. As a preliminary exercise the following type of drill is useful:

c is 1 in C major and c minor
c is 2 in B♭ major and minor
c is 3 in A♭ major and a minor
c is 4 in G major and minor
c is 5 in F major and minor
c is 6 in E♭ major and e minor
c is 7 in D♭ major and, enharmonically, b♯ is seven in c♯ minor

The black note above c is best known as 1 in D♭ major or c♯ minor, etc. An index with its locations should be correct in all details. The use of large letters for Major and small letters for minor saves time, and the use of correct symbols for each kind of triad trains accurate reading and hearing. The complete statement for the last chord in the index of C is e-g♯-b♯, better known than the enharmonic notation f♭, a♭ and c; it is an augmented triad found on III in the key of c♯ minor. Each chord should find its place in the total system. If it does not, there is some error in spelling or location. Anyone who knows the scales from which the chords are derived can benefit from this study of vocabulary, without the aid of a teacher of harmony.

Although this triad-index is only a small part of a much larger index, it can be used in root positions or inversions to free the student from the bonds of a single tonality in improvisation and composition; for instance, in the index of A, he can have: F, A$_4^6$, d, d♭ (aug. triad), F$_4^6$, a^6, D, f♯, etc.

After he is familiar with the twelve triads of each index he may add the diatonic sevenths, i.e., a major or a minor third on top of the constructions already pictured (ex. 82). This would produce eight pictures;

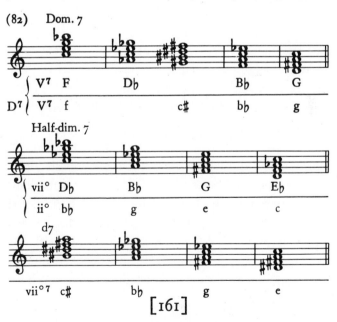

(82)   Dom. 7

m⁷				

ii⁷	B♭	G	E♭	C
iii⁷	A♭	F	D♭	B♭
vi⁷	E♭	C	A♭	F
(with Low L.T.) i⁷	c	a	f	d
iv⁷	g	e	c	a

M⁷				

I⁷	C	A♭	F	D♭
IV⁷	G	E♭	C	A♭
(with Low L.T.) III⁷	a	f	d	b♭
VI⁷	e	c	a	f

but the major third on top of the augmented triad merely doubles the sound of the root, so that there are only seven new sounds. As suggested in the chapter on sevenths I have stressed only five of these. In the order of their introduction in most texts we add them to the index: (1) the dominant seventh, (2) the half-diminished seventh, found on the leading-tone of the major mode and on the supertonic of the minor mode, (3) the diminished seventh, (4) minor sevenths, and (5) major sevenths. Some theorists number these: 7^1, 7^2, etc., but their names with the exception of (2) are short and can be spoken quickly for ready identification in dictation. The dominant sevenths are named for their location. The symbol D^7 would distinguish the sound as different from those using large numerals: I^7, etc. Names are immaterial but the identification of individual sound character is all-important.

The two sevenths omitted from the index as given (i^7 and III^{+7}) were not used as diatonic sevenths in the common-practice period (the i^7 had to wait for Scriabin's seventh piano sonata for its "diatonic" treatment). More profitable would be the addition to the index of the dominant ninths, with both minor and major ninths, there being ten of these. If desired, other ninths: ii^9, vi^9, iii^9, IV^9, etc., can be added; however, in the classroom I have usually stopped the index after the dominant ninths. The student will be able to find many illustrations even in this limited index of the fact that any two chords go well in succession.

One of the most famous illustrations of this chapter in all music is the art-song *A Monotone* (*Ein Ton*) by Cornelius, in which the voice sings throughout the one note of an index. The reader may be interested in classifying all the harmonies which appear in this song. He will find only one ninth chord, and it is worth noting that this most complicated chord used by Cornelius, a dominant minor ninth, occurs about three-fourths of the way through the song, i.e., at the same relative point as that at which the climax occurs

in classical drama. Purcell's Five-part Fantasia in
which the viola plays one note throughout is another
famous illustration. An amusing composition for
band by Percy Grainger, *Immovable Do* or *Cyphering
C,* is based entirely on the index of C which we have
given. This last title reminds us that the organist who
is bothered by a cypher during the prelude might find
the index a "present help in trouble": however, the
real value of the plurisignificance of tones is in shorter
periods, with frequent shifting of the note indexed.

An excerpt from Liszt's *Les Préludes* is an illustration:

(83)

same four measures
in E-flat, ending:

Moussorgsky has been able to produce many remark-
able effects with only two dominant sevenths of an

index in the extended pages introducing the Corona-
tion Scene in *Boris Godunov*.

Practice resulting in a thorough acquaintance with
the twelve indices and their use in improvisations and
chance association introduces the student to more modern styles in which all chords are considered related. The indices can suggest a variety of choices
at any point in the writing of a song, for instance.
The melodic note for the next word may be clearly
in mind, but exactly the right connotation of supporting harmony or the particular "color" desired
may be but vaguely heard or not so clearly dictated.
The entire index of the melody note may be played
through the inner, or if necessary, the outer ear, until
the combination sought, or but vaguely heard, is
reached. The early use of an index frees the student
from a single tonality and suggests modulations far
beyond the usual five related keys.

Thus far we have given only the diatonic locations
of the chords in the indices. After chromatic harmony is studied, the location of these same chords
when used as the clichés of the five generalizations
can be added (see next chapter). For instance, the
first triad, c-e-g, is a Neapolitan in B major or b
minor, a second dominant in B♭ major or minor, a
third dominant in E♭ major or minor, etc. The
half-diminished seventh, c-e♭-g♭-b♭ is not only dia-

tonic in Db major and bb minor but is a borrowed "menacing" effect in Bb major and a satellite or attendant pre-cadence effect in Gb major. Dominant sevenths may be located as German augmented sixths, etc. (cf. the next chapter).

For use in an index of possible harmonies, it is absolutely necessary that the note which is being indexed be not altered in location. When students start to write, this is likely to be forgotten. Emphasize that this change of place makes the index as useless as a dictionary in which the words beginning with B are mixed up with those beginning with A. The note may be changed enharmonically, and in vocal or orchestral performance the actual number of vibrations may change slightly, but in equal temperament it is represented by the same key on the piano. To be sure, in modern composition, adjacent indices are used, or the note of one becomes an appoggiatura to the note of another; what has just been said concerns merely the vocabulary. The order given, the historical order, is the order of increasing dissonance and the order of probable use; and there is some slight value in keeping a uniform order for facility in survey and for possible selections.

While it is true that there are not thirty-two different sounds in the index of triads and sevenths just given, the ambiguity or similarity of certain sounds has its own advantages. Each diminished seventh sounds like an inversion of the other three, and so, by enharmonic change, is at home in four tonalities — and, by the major-minor generalization, in a total of eight keys. There are only three such sounds in all music; yet they are also found as attendant or satellite chords to the primary triads of every key, i.e., one each around I, IV and V. No wonder any diminished seventh chord may be inserted, if desired, anywhere; thus, the twenty-four Preludes of Chopin or Shostakovitch make multiple use of these three sound combinations. There are also four augmented triads, with many different spellings but with only one sound in each index.

Familiarity with the indices aids harmonic analysis and sight-reading. As an assignment, they are excellent "medicine" for the student who is having difficulty in harmony due to the lack of thorough acquaintance with *all* tonalities. This lack is particularly prevalent in respect to the harmonic minor mode and its chords. Theoretical knowledge of an index is not enough; there should be the highest possible degree of facility with the combinations at tongue and finger tips. Too often facility as one of the important goals in the study of harmony is neglected. In composition, it is true that we do not ordinarily ask whether a work is finished in a day or a year, and yet a certain readiness of vocabulary should assist in registering the flow of musical ideas. The tempo of performance in the class-room is quite important.

The removal of upper strata or melodic decoration reduces tonal music to these fundamental harmonies; even elaborate chromatic harmonies usually first appear as melodic decoration. Most chromatic harmonies entered music as modifications of diatonic effects, and often the chromatic effect is merely a diatonic effect located on another degree; for instance, the Neapolitan effect, to be discussed in the next chapter, consists of two major triads a half-step apart (usually placed in their first inversion to avoid parallel fifths). It is found quite "at home," diatonically, between VI and V of the minor mode. This attractive effect when transferred to other locations is considered chromatic because it involves accidentals in these locations. Recognition and understanding of well-known chromatic effects (which we will generalize in the next discussion) are therefore dependent upon recognition of the fundamental diatonic sounds. Actually sections on chromatic harmony in the usual textbook contain very few sounds that are different from those of our index. Until a musician is able to sing in arpeggio-form, as well as play and write rapidly, all the harmonies of these indices, he will still find it useful to practice them as a means of developing general musicianship. From the standpoint of today's music, all tonalities and all chords are related to each other; thus the use of these indices which cut across the old barriers between tonalities affords a good introduction to many modern effects. We need familiarity with harmonic words to prevent painful note-by-note reading. Facility has been a chief goal in the teaching of performance but is too often neglected in the teaching of theory.

Fortunately, there is not the same danger from harmonic combinations that there is in the chemical laboratory, and the student should be encouraged to experiment with the newer additions to the index. The composer is free to do as he pleases; only his musical instinct, something like the Quakers' Inner Light, is his guide — he hopes to find someone else who will like what he pleases to do. Freedom within continuously enlarging fields is the best policy in the classroom. The student might be encouraged to add to the many variations on "Chopsticks" written by the Russian Five. Liszt contributed an additional one but there are many possibilities in more modern idioms which this theme can employ. With the theme on the fixed position of the white notes, the original set employs C, G, F, a, d and other tonalities. The plurisignificance of a pattern of several notes is also illustrated in the *Lament* in Honegger's *King David*. Indices are related to pedal points and basso ostinatos, but these two devices are usually discussed in a chapter near the end of a text whereas the index of triads should be introduced at least as soon as all triads in root position are being considered.

CHAPTER XI

Chromatic Clichés

Conventional chromatic harmony can be summarized to a considerable extent in one series of chords placed before a cadence:

(84)

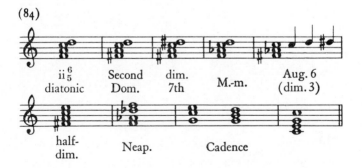

These have been used so often that they have become clichés. I remember being present at a discussion of the teaching of harmony, during which a composer said: "Why do we spend so much time teaching the augmented sixth effects when I have to say to my students in composition, 'Why use such threadbare progressions'?" The less time we spend upon what the typical text spreads over several chapters, the better. Any *one* or all or any number of the above pre-cadence chords may go directly to the cadence (there are innumerable illustrations). To be sure, they can be used in other inversions or in root position. The second inversion, $\frac{4}{3}$, shows the augmented sixth chords in their more characteristic position:

(85)

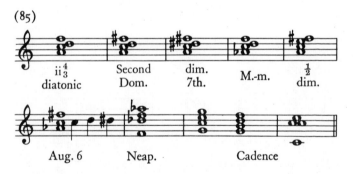

ii$\frac{4}{3}$
diatonic

Second
Dom.

dim.
7th.

M.-m.

$\frac{1}{2}$
dim.

Aug. 6   Neap.   Cadence

This presents an empirical or practical approach through alterations of the supertonic or subdominant triads and sevenths. Note that there is only one new sound in this line, the French Augmented Sixth, a♭, c, d, f♯, containing two dissonances. The rest are sounds already present in the indices of Chapter X: dominant sevenths, half-diminished and diminished sevenths, or major triads.

While these effects are most frequently found in the pre-cadence position as alterations of ii or IV, they can be found on any other position, i.e., as alterations of vi before ii, or of iii before vi.

(86)

dim.⁷   half.-dim.⁷   ii°⁷   Neap. 6th   Second dom.

Aug. 6th   ii   I⁶₄ V   I

Now let us approach these chromatically altered chords in more detail by means of five generalizations:

[173]

1. Outside of every triad, as a "satellite," is a diminished seventh (and a half-diminished seventh).
2. Any chord in a minor key may be used in its parallel major. We may call the result a major-minor mode.
3. Above (and below) every triad there are chromatic "slip-chord" effects, the most famous one being the "Neapolitan sixth." (For an extended explanation of the slip-chord see Section III following.)
4. Before any triad there is a chain of dominants. This is a complete circle of first conjugations, but because of the augmented fourth between IV and vii, the series usually stops with the fifth dominant.
5. Inside every octave of the scale there are augmented sixth effects which "explode" to that octave.

As already stated, these effects are usually related to the dominant, before which they stand in the precadence position; but they are being used in many other locations at present, and it is important to emphasize the "any" and "every" in these five statements.

Let us now take up these generalizations one by one.

Chromatic Clichés

I. Accompanying every triad in each tonality there is an attendant diminished-seventh chord which may serve as a satellite-chord, attracted to the triad and collapsing or resolving to it.

This particular chromatic effect is "born" (i.e., is diatonic) in the relationship of vii°-i of the minor mode:

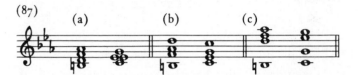

(87)   (a)   (b)   (c)

The three good methods of resolving this third-class progression are all given above on one staff: (a) doubled third to avoid parallel fifths, (b) doubled root with fauxbourbon effect of parallel thirds and sixths in the three upper voices, and (c) a less usual, but possible, doubling of the fifth. We remember these methods from the chapter on seventh chords. As is usual in the history of harmony an effect which is diatonic or "at home" in one location can be moved to other locations. Through use of the "Tierce de Picardie" (cf., the second generalization listed above), it came to be used on the leading-tone of the parallel major mode, and from there to be found in all locations:

(88)

Although this sequence does not leave the key of
C major, each diminished seventh may be spelled
and played as though it were in the key of the triad
it attends. After playing the sequence in all keys
the student may use these chords as accompaniment
for melodic patterns, a waltz, for instance. V_5^6 is
substituted for the poorer vii° in the final cadence.
Think of each successive triad as a new tonic, and
remember that the leading-tone on which the effect
is "born" is but a half-step below this tonic, with the
seventh chord wearing the minor signature of the
same tonic. However, it should be emphasized that
this sequence does not, or need not, modulate: it is
merely a chain of third-class progressions in their
best or most usual directions, with diminished-
seventh satellites to each, as the Roman numerals
I, ii, iii, etc., indicate. The bass is a chromatic scale

[176]

except at the one point between iii and IV **where**
only a half-step occurs and where the root of **iii**
must be repeated as the root of the diminished
seventh attendant to IV.

Next, these chromatic diminished seventh effects
will be illustrated in second-class progressions moving
in the usual direction:

(89)

I   vi   IV   ii

and in first-class progressions, also in the usual direction:

(90)

iii   vi⁶   ii   V⁶

They are not always used at such length or in sequences. One modification in spelling at the pre-

[177]

cadence position should be discussed as it is used in the series of chromatic effects with which the chapter began. When the satellite to the dominant proceeds to a major-tonic $^6_4$, it is usually respelled:

(91)

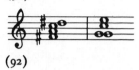

Beethoven sometimes spells this effect as a diminished seventh around the dominant even when the major follows:

(92)

Transposed and reduced from Beethoven's *Piano Sonata*, Op. 31, No. 3, first movement, measures 5-6 (and many other sources).

although this requires two accidentals instead of one in this upper voice.

A defense of his spelling, explained as the top of a supertonic dominant ninth, is the main thesis of the book *Die Geheimdokumente der Davidsbündler* by Giovanni Minotti. The theoretically correct spelling avoids one accidental and agrees with the conventional treatment of the chromatic scale, in which rising accidentals are used in ascent. In a minor key the spelling of ex. 92 is retained for both V and i^6_4.

II. The second generalization concerning chromatic effects emphasizes the fact that C major and c minor have more in common in some respects than C major and its relative minor:

Chromatic Clichés

Any chord used in a minor key is chromatically effective and satisfactory in its parallel major key.

The historical basis for this generalization reaches so far back in the history of the art that a thorough discussion would require many pages. In barest outline it may be represented thus:

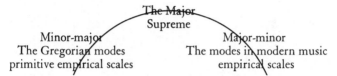

The Major
Supreme

Minor-major   Major-minor
The Gregorian modes   The modes in modern music
primitive empirical scales   empirical scales

Modern music seems to be repeating in reverse order some of the processes of an earlier cycle. The modes in their theoretically pure forms were early modified by *musica ficta,* and compositions were brought to a close with a chord in which if the third appeared at all it was a major third. This effect, later called "tierce de Picardie," may explain the ease with which certain chords in the minor mode have been used in the major mode, for it is logically but a short step from (a) to (b) in the following illustration:

(93)   (a)   (b)

"Tierce de Picardie" in c minor   C major

However, this step is so important that it may be considered typical of what might be called in modern music a major-minor mode with an emphasis upon the hyphen as a bridge between two modes built upon the same tonic. The peculiar effect of the first chord in (b) has been given the name "menacing effect" by Franklin W. Robinson in his *Aural Harmony,* with the purpose of aiding students to recognize this chromatic effect through psychological means. There are many more chromatic borrowings that may be classified under this generalization:

(94)

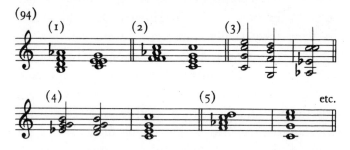

In (1) we see why the diminished seventh is at home in both modes. The minor subdominant (2), and in fact many chords involving the lowered sixth of the scale, have a sentimental emotional effect much used in Italian opera of the last two centuries. The deceptive cadence to a lowered submediant also falls in this generalization. The mediant of c minor (4) appears spelled enharmonically as V with a raised fifth. (5) is the "menacing seventh" in its most famous inversion as a chord of the added sixth. Other illustrations might easily be added.

III. The third chromatic generalization concerns the famous Neapolitan effect (the derivation of the name is obscure but may refer to the Neapolitan school of opera which made use of such chords). It is generally known as the Neapolitan *sixth* because it usually appeared in its first inversion. This use of fauxbourdon with a tonic following prevented the appearance of consecutive fifths; however, the chord also appears in root position and in second inversion, and for that reason it is better to call it the Neapolitan effect. Concerning its use the following generalization can be made: a major triad or its inversion may appear a half-step above and/or below any triad of the scale.

Usually this effect is said to be a major triad on the lowered supertonic but we may cover a wider field of more modern effects by means of the above generalization. The effect was "born" between two major chords which are a half-step apart in the minor mode:

(95)

VI⁶   V⁶

Again the discovery of an effective relationship led to its being tried in other locations — whether through accident or logical experiment it would be difficult to say. There is here a reasonable similarity to procedure in scientific invention (although we should not suggest that composition in an art is merely the result of scientific logic). For example, in 1934 a team of scientists discovered the bactericidal effects of sulfanilamide. By experimentation the grouping of the elements within the compound was changed by various substituent groups to produce over a thousand variations of the parent compound, some of which had enhanced bactericidal properties over the parent sulfanilamide.

After long experimental or intuitive use, a musical generalization is made possible. At the risk of too sweeping a generalization, for the sake of an effective summary of the third chromatic effect, we may repeat that the Neapolitan chord can be used above and below all triads. The latter position, below the following triad, is less frequently used and has not been included under the name of the effect heretofore. Its use is increasing, and the method of slipping any chord or its inversion down or up by half or whole steps has been greatly expanded in the twentieth century. For such effects we have found the term "slip-chords" useful although this betrays their frequent appearance in popular music and in such work as the following end of John Alden Carpenter's *Krazey-Kat Ballet*:

(96)

The better-known (descending) Neapolitan effect may be practiced in the following sequence:

(97) (a)

Simply play a chromatic succession of major first inversions in the right hand, and at any point introduce a cadential $^6_4$. Each chord is a "Neapolitan" to the one below it; this can be proved by having students make a cadence at any point in the series. In the example the cadence has been made in C major (or in c minor if we use the accidentals in parenthesis), but it could just as well have been made one chord later in B major or b minor. Practice stopping at any point by adding a cadence I^6_4-V-I in the key represented by a root a half-step lower than the root of the last chromatic inversion in the chain.

It is true that Arthur Foote and W. R. Spalding (in *Modern Harmony,* for instance) taught two such effects, one on the lowered supertonic, a half-step

above the keynote, and the other *on* the supertonic,
a major triad a whole step above the tonic. Some
writers add confusion to confusion by calling this a
"German Neapolitan" sixth. It is much better to
disassociate these two effects and consider the "German Neapolitan" a *second* dominant, or dominant
of the dominant, as a part of a chain of such dominants which is basic for our fourth generalization:

IV. Chromatic dominant effects may form a complete circle of first class progressions.

Each step in the first class progression circle:

(98)

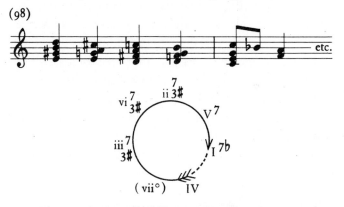

may be recognized as the dominant degree of the
next step in the direction of the arrow, and each
step may be made a real dominant by chromatic
alterations (in the major mode all that is necessary
is the raising of the third of the triads iii, vi and ii;

[185]

in minor more alterations are required). To these
simple triads may be added minor sevenths, producing dominant seventh sounds for each step of the
circle; or, ninths and elevenths may rise on the same
degrees. These structures can be chromatically altered
— the fifth raised or lowered, etc. In fact, they are generally so altered in popular music, to disguise the fact
that the "music goes round and 'round" a limited circle of progressions in that idiom. Because students are
so familiar with the second, third and fourth dominants in dance music it is sometimes advisable for the
teacher to use illustrations that are colloquial and "at
hand" in the side of a student's life which we sometimes try to ignore. Rather than leading to a love of
jazz and its increased use, a little harmonic analysis
often shows the harmony class the underlying poverty
of harmonic progression in that style. On our school
campuses, traditional folk-songs and group-songs offer
additional illustrations. The following is from a fra-
ternity song well known on many a college campus:

(99)

These effects are not necessarily "colloquial"; consider the beginning of the second subject of Mozart's *Symphony in G Minor:*

(100)

These illustrations show chords proceeding immediately from the initial tonic to the fourth dominant and then successively through the third, second, and first dominant seventh to a cadence in the tonic. To state this in terms of the first illustration above (ex. 99), the second chord b-d♯-f♯-a is the dominant seventh of E, but when the next chord arrives, we find an added d♮ which produces the dominant seventh of A; similarly, when A major arrives, g♮ is added to form the dominant seventh of D, which is the dominant of the main key. The second dominant is often termed the "dominant-of-the-dominant," but this becomes cumbersome when we have to speak of the "dominant of the dominant of the dominant of the dominant"; so it is better to call this "great-great-grandfather" the fourth dominant (in a sense, the tonic or "son," the present-tense generation, follows the dominant or "father"; ii is the "grandfather," etc.). Only by thinking of first-class progressions as a complete chain or circle do we see some relationships in longer spans, and avoid referring too frequently to the "dominant of the mediant," etc. In popular music the second dominant is a chromatic "barber-shop"* effect, and the series seldom reaches farther back than the fourth dominant.

That the circle is actually a complete one may be illustrated by the following excerpt from Chopin: (101)

Chopin, *Mazurka*, Op. 17, No. 1, measures 15-17

*This term probably goes back to Elizabethan days when the barber was the surgeon and music the only anesthetic.

Teaching Music Theory

Circles of first-class progressions may begin and end at any point, for they are trains such as those around the Ringstrasse in Vienna, which you may enter and leave at any station; at each musical station you may transfer or modulate to outlying keys.

When practicing these sequences—and indeed, all others given in earlier installments, you can add interest by playing the harmonic foundation in the left hand, forming some familiar pattern such as the after-beats of waltz rhythm; then improvise an added melody in the right hand. This melody can be completely sequential:

(102)

However, a sequence becomes almost unbearable after three repetitions; longer circles should be made more interesting by a change in the melodic pattern:

(103)

etc.

(after fourth measure of Ex. 102)

A complete change of melodic pattern in each measure is possible because of the unity of the harmonic sequence, but less melodic unity would result; and a certain amount of melodic sequence is typical of these progressions as they have so often been used in actual compositions.

V.   The fifth and last chromatic effect may be stated in the following generalization:

Inside every octave of every scale there are augmented-sixth effects which "explode" to that octave.

Instead of seeking the theoretical derivation of these effects as chromatic alterations of diatonic chords, we would do better from a practical standpoint to become familiar with augmented-sixth effects both at the keyboard and aurally before proceeding to theoretical terminology. Although they come from many different sources, they have but one characteristic "explosive" effect. If the reader is already familiar with theoretical explanations of augmented sixths, discussion of this generalization may assist him in reviewing their effect; if he is not, he need not be deterred from acquiring a practical acquaintance with these same effects.

The heart of the effect is in the two voices which explode the augmented sixth, from which the name is derived, to an octave:

(104)

I ii iii IV V

This effect may be played inside all octaves of the chromatic scale, or inside the octaves of a diatonic scale of any tonality, provided some attention is given to the spelling. These effects are often misspelled, particularly in popular music. Unless the explosion occurs or is understood to occur it is useless to name or spell an augmented sixth. In such cases as the following, however, the c♮ of the second chord is but a substitute for the d which is omitted, and from which it would have passed, and the augmented sixth may still be heard:

(105)

Of course the augmented sixth effect may just as readily appear in other positions. When inverted it might be called the "diminished third" effect, which now collapses to an octave or unison. Frequently both occur in the works of classical composers as embellishments

(106)

of the octave (ex. 106, often found in Mozart's works). Having become familiar with the important outlines of the effect (its exterior surfaces, or perhaps we should say, its explosive fuses, since these need not occur in outer voices), we are now ready to generalize concerning the inner content or remaining members of the harmonies. An ultra-modern generalization would be the following:

Within the augmented sixth or diminished third and within its octave resolution *anything* may occur.

This is a sweeping generalization but it is literally true of present-day music. The following is a relatively simple illustration, which appears at first to be

[193]

elaborate: play a glissando on the white keys of the piano for any number of octaves, starting with G and ending with f; follow this with an elbow-chord, *à la* Henry Cowell, on all the black keys within this compass and you have an augmented sixth effect which could be used even for a coloristic final cadence, since g-f is really g-e♯ and both harmonies have by-tones. A still more violent tone-cluster of all the black and white notes inside an octave could be used for the augmented sixth, provided the notes of the final octave were heard as an explosion of this cluster. This most extreme extension of the generalization is not recommended!

To summarize conventional use of the augmented sixth, we may state that the octave resolution is used as root, third, or fifth of either major or minor triads. This may be stated in other words: the chord of resolution is usually a major or minor triad, in root position or inversion. The content of the augmented sixth is here given in figured bass:

(107)

"Italian" "French" "German"

Chromatic Clichés

In this condensed outline of the effect, whole notes are used for the notes common to all, quarter-notes for the variants. Any one of the augmented chords may go to any one of the resolutions. Not to be left out of this game of national nicknames, some English theorists call the enharmonic spelling of the German Aug. $\frac{6+}{5}_3$ the English augmented sixth (with doubly augmented fourth, $\frac{6}{4}_3{}_{++}$). The figured bass symbols look complicated; however, the sounds of the Italian and German effects are those of a dominant seventh, incomplete and complete respectively; the only new sound of these most-used combinations is the double-dissonant sound of the French augmented sixth. These effects are closely related to the Neapolitan chord of our third generalization; the dominant seventh heard in the Italian and German augmented sixths is the dominant seventh of the Neapolitan chord considered as tonic. Also, the resolution of the German augmented sixth to a triad on the dominant contains major triads a half-step apart; this is the Neapolitan effect in its diatonic location, VI-V of the minor mode.

Using the generalization that *anything* may fill the augmented sixth, we secure a number of important variants which are not usually included in text-books although they are used by Elgar, R. Strauss, and even Wagner. When we remember that the interval of the augmented sixth is the same as a minor seventh, we may expect the other two of the five sounds of seventh chords to be used, exploding as augmented sixths:

(108)

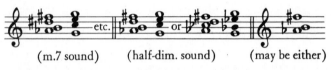

  (m.7 sound) (half-dim. sound) (may be either)

The complete whole-tone scale can be used between the notes of the augmented sixth, or any part of that scale is possible:

(109)

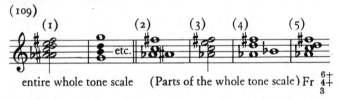

entire whole tone scale (Parts of the whole tone scale) Fr $\frac{6+}{4+}$
3

In the above classification we note the sound of dominant sevenths with a raised fifth in (3) and (4). The sound of the dominant seventh with a lowered fifth was already present in the French augmented sixth.

The chromatic effects and their various locations can be included in the index discussed in the last chapter; i.e., as augmented sixth effects, dominant

[196]

sevenths are used in many chromatic locations in addition to their diatonic locations. The French augmented sixth and all the whole-tone "fillers" of the last illustration have pluri-significance. The augmented sixth chord in ex. 110:

is inside the dominant octave of the key of C and when spelled enharmonically is inside the dominant octave of F♯ or G♭ (ex. 111):

(110)

(111)

Actually this chord stresses the modern dominant by its augmented fourth. The entire whole-tone scale, being composed of whole steps which are equivalent to diminished thirds (aug. 6ths), may resolve or "explode" to five different octaves (cf. Chapter XII).

Before all this becomes too complicated, let me again emphasize the pragmatic approach at the keyboard. Your students can easily play and spell the outside interval, which expands to the octave, moving like electricity over the smallest step on the piano. The major third above the bottom of the chord is present in all the four usual spellings. That third is doubled in the Italian and may move in a series of passing notes through the special French and German-English notes. A practical approach at the keyboard is best for this and all chromatic generalizations. It is true that the same effects may be approached by the addition of accidentals to the scale and its diatonic chords, but so many different Roman numerals with so many alterations are required that an empirical approach using the five generalizations given above is better. As in a spoken language, a knowledge of the derivation of words is interesting, but every day we use many words whose derivation we do not know or do not stop to consider. In the conventional augmented sixth effects we have only two sounds, that of a strange or remote dominant seventh and the new double-dissonant sound.

Although we have stated, in this last generalization concerning augmented sixth chords, that they appear inside *every* octave, it is a good idea to emphasize again the fact that they usually appear inside the *dominant* octave in the typical text. If the student knows the tonality he is in or to which he is modulating, he will find the augmented sixth inside the dominant octave of that key all he will need in the harmonization of basses or sopranos in most textbooks. This is the pre-cadence position; however, it is also a good idea to use them in sequences of all three conjugations:

Chromatic Clichés

(112)

ii   V   I

First Conjugation

(113)

Second Conjugation

(114)

Third Conjugation

The works of Gilbert and Sullivan afford illustrations of all five chromatic generalizations. Popular music is full of these clichés; the 28 variations on Stephen Foster's *Old Folks at Home,* (published by Marks) by 28 "composers" who were popular in Tin-Pan Alley, might interest your students. Some acquaintance with these chords as used in popular music makes all the more astonishing the fact that in the hands of great composers these clichés do not sound as though they had been worn threadbare.

The arrow-directions continue to hold and remain valid regardless of the structures which are erected upon them. An excellent example may be found in the beginning of Brahms' *Intermezzo* in bb minor, Op. 117, No. 2, where the composer goes entirely around the circle from tonic to tonic using diatonic seventh chords. The tonality is minor; these sequences are exactly like those in the parallel major except that the raised leading-tone is used from the final dominant to tonic to prove that we have been in minor all the time but have used the lowered leading-tone elsewhere. In the next two lines Brahms goes over the same ground again but this time with a chain of dominant sevenths, that is, each one of the secondary sevenths has been chromatically altered into a dominant seventh of the next step which follows. Toward the end of this same *Intermezzo* we have a series of chromatic dominant sevenths a half step apart in which each dominant seventh may really be an augmented sixth inside an octave for which another seventh substitutes. The last one Brahms does spell as an augmented sixth to bring the series to a close on the following octave.

[200]

Chromatic Clichés

Most of the chromatic effects which may be discovered by the student in the music which he is studying or memorizing will come under one of these five categories:

Outside every triad, a satellite diminished seventh;
The major-minor mode;
Inside every octave, an explosive augmented sixth;
Above or below every triad, a Neapolitan slip-chord effect;
Before all triads, a chain of dominants.

Thought and attention given to these generalizations should improve facility in sight-reading and memorization. Theory is useless unless used!

We have now covered the most important considerations of harmonic theory. Let us now return to our division of vocabulary into Pre-cadence, Cadence and Final, or IV, V, and I, and suggest modulation first to nearly related keys and then to those more distant, using a formula of seven chords:

1. The tonic of the initial key (considered to be established);
2. The dominant seventh of the new key or one of its inversions;
3. The resolution of this dominant seventh to the new tonic;
4. A pre-cadence chord chosen from the diatonic: IV, IV^6, ii, ii^6, I^6, VI, II^7 and its inversions,

etc., or from the chromatic clichés discussed in this chapter;

5. Tonic $^6_4$;
6. Dominant seventh or iii^6, with all its connotations of a dominant thirteenth, etc.;
7. Tonic of the final key.

By focusing the attention of the performer and the ears of the rest of the class upon the dominant seventh of the new key and upon the various choices of the fourth item, the pre-cadence chord, we set up an excellent problem involving three of the important objectives discussed in the first chapter. The methods of modulating from one key to another are perhaps infinite; however, they all involve the "clinching" of the modulation by a cadence in the new home established, we might almost say, by support from the left and the right, pre-cadence and cadence. Examiners of the American Guild of Organists have commented upon the fact that so many players are able to get to the new key but so few able to prove that they have arrived. Individual written orders for specific modulations involving the use of specific pre-cadence chords afford not only keyboard drill for one student but ear problems for all the rest. The type of pre-cadence chord demanded would, of course, depend upon the maturity of the class. Students who have been using the tonal center or the leading tone to identify all diatonic harmonies have only to watch the behavior of the tonal center when the new dominant seventh is heard. For modulations to the five nearest related keys: The tonic of a major key becomes the seventh of the V^7 of the dominant key and the root of V^7 of the subdominant. It descends a half-step to become the fifth of V^7 of the relative minor or the root of V^7 of the mediant. It rises a half step to become the third of V^7 of the supertonic, completing the five keys most closely related. From the tonic of a minor key the same changes to dominant and subdominant keys occur as in major. However, for the other three most important modulations different changes occur; the old center moves up or down a whole-step to become third or root respectively of V^7 in the relative major (III), up a half-step to become the seventh of V^7 in the submediant major (VI), and holds over to become the fifth of V^7 in a major key on the low leading-tone (VII). All of this sounds more complicated than it is in application, provided the student can quickly sing or hear in his imagination the one dominant seventh of the index that agrees with the chord being played when the new key is entered.

To secure a response from each member of the class, I suggest the use of the five fingers while the eyes are shut: four fingers for the modulation to the subdominant, five for the dominant; then if we use one finger for the relative major or relative minor, we have two and three fingers left for the supertonic and mediant minors representing the distances above an initial major key, and for the majors on the lowered leading-tone and on the submediant, representing the distance below an initial minor key. There is no question that with the passing of each year it is more and more important that the principles of conventional harmony or common practice be understood and mastered in as short a time as possible. The main purpose of the chapters thus far has been to offer suggestions which facilitate such understanding. Rather than aim at the inclusion of every detail I have explained only the most important procedures and generalizations. It is hoped that with this background the student can take up the fascinating features of twentieth-century harmony.

CHAPTER XII

Harmony in the Twentieth Century

THEORY is a notorious laggard. Are there any suggestions we can offer our students that will help
to bring some order out of the seeming confusion in
contemporary music? If there has been a progressive
and creative attitude in the classroom throughout the
period of instruction, students will not be unprepared
for complete freedom of action. The composer has
only his artistic conscience or "inner light" to guide
him. He must believe in the products of his imagination and hope to find others who will believe
in them. If he is still in a classroom, his teacher and

his fellow classmates can serve as critics and represent a more or less enlightened segment of the general public when they state their reactions to his work. A student is even more ready to listen to the opinions of fellow students than to those of his teacher who presumably represents an older generation. We as teachers should be careful not to discourage any ideas which students present and, if they are able, perform with conviction. We may need to point out those features which from the standpoint of our own artistic conscience stray too far from the norm, but we should be sure that our opinion is based upon a wide knowledge of very early and very recent music. We will be particularly fortunate if we find among our students several who like to experiment with combinations of musical sound. Most biographies of composers describe groups of young musicians, often with little or no formal instruction, vying with each other in producing interesting work for mutual encouragement and criticism. When this situation is fostered in the classroom the teacher should try to be a "contemporary" of the rest, possibly one with a wider perspective.

In this book I have emphasized the primacy of rhythm. With rhythm and melody alone much can be said in a style truly contemporary. While this approach represents a return to fundamentals it does so with a difference which makes the result new. Let us frankly admit that much of the lush harmonic color of nineteenth-century music is dated and will be stigmatized in the future as all too characteristic of that period — or perhaps it will remain localized *ad nauseum* in Hollywood. The 19th century was the period of harmonic exploitation to an extraordinary degree. The best composers of the present day show a lack of interest in the kind of harmony we have been teaching; on the other hand, there has been a logical extension of the idea of melodic line.

As a beginning exercise we might start with a line of plainsong and then treat it in: (a) parallel thirds (gymel), (b) parallel octaves and fifths (organum), (c) parallel triads in root position, (d) parallel first inversions, (e) parallel second inversions, (f) chords with added sixths, (g) pan-diatonic or white-note tone clusters, (h) more complex tone-clusters including all notes within certain limits (seconds, thirds, fourths, fifths, etc.). Regardless of the chords used — successive diminished sevenths, half-diminished sevenths, minor sevenths, major sevenths, etc. — we still have only a *melody,* or one melodic line, in various disguises or costumes. However, we have in this paragraph many of the devices used by important composers today. Randall Thompson is particularly fond of the fauxbourdon of second inversions:

[207]

(115)

Randall Thompson, *Alleluia* (m.58-59)

To be sure this device was used by the great "modernist", J. S. Bach, generally over a pedal point. Shostakovitch uses it *under* a pedal point in his *Quintet,* Op. 57:

(116)

Shostakovitch, *Quintet,* Op. 52,
First movement (meas. 2)

End of meas. 12
(root positions)

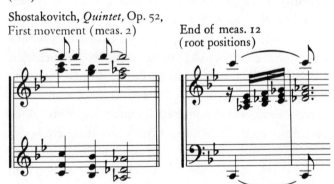

Harmony in the Twentieth Century

If the reader has been critical of the time spent in this book upon rhythm without melody or melody without harmony, I can give no better illustration or justification for a return to these essentials than the work of Carl Orff. In the opera-cantata *Carmina Burana,* which is his best-known work in this country, one might say with only a little exaggeration that there are no harmonic progressions. There are only originality and vitality of rhythm plus interesting melodies treated in some of the ways listed above. The melodies are single-line in the style of plain-song or folk-tunes; there are oriental arabesques in a sort of coloratura, as well as strands treated as in (a) to (h) above (p. 207), but there is little harmonic progression beyond a division by the dominant. Contrasting tonalities are to be found, and certain patterns may be seen in the arrangement of these tonalities (cf. Ingeborg Kiekert in *Die Musikalische Form in den Werken Carl Orffs,* [Regensburg; Gustav Bosse Verlag, 1957], but this composer does not demand in his listeners a knowledge of the romantic, chromatic effects of the nineteenth century. Although the ultimate importance of Orff's music is still being debated, it would not be a bad idea to acquaint your students with his work early in their course as proof of the fact that they need not wait for a knowledge of conventional

[209]

harmonic progressions before they begin to create.

When two melodic lines are used we enter the field of counterpoint, a field we have not as yet discussed to any extent. In present-day music if the two lines are logical and consistent in themselves as chordal complexes, even when amplified in any of the ways listed above, they must be assumed to fit together.

(117)

As we approach the teaching of twentieth-century harmony we will do well to continue using the principles, generalizations and methods developed for the chromatic harmony of the nineteenth century as long as they result in clarity or efficiency. This is possible even with music which was once thought to approach atonality. As in musical form so also in harmony there has been not a revolution but rather an evolution; moreover, the older ways of looking at music are imbedded in our logical thought processes and have at least the value of habit and custom. We do not so quickly discard the established patterns of harmonic relationships.

We cannot discuss or generalize without analysis and careful study of the musical style we are considering; this means that we must know a style intimately, and one of the best ways to be sure that we know a work well is to memorize it. But the problem is circular; to memorize, unless we painfully record each note separately, we must generalize, and that involves analysis. In all music, and particularly in that of the twentieth century, a most important question is one that asks: What is a chord or harmony? We may take two extreme positions: (1) Heinrich Schenker's method which ends logically in one chord or one harmony for an entire composition assumed to be tonal, or (2) the method which selects a short time unit, perhaps the quarter-note, and names the structures of thirds at each time-unit. Somewhere between these two extremes is the position of Walter Piston as he discusses harmonic rhythm, but nowhere does he state exactly what chords or progressions he will accept in his rhythmic design. On page 41 of his *Harmony* Piston suggests an "open minded appraisal of the rhythmic values of each individual musical phrase" and on page 47 he states:

"The rhythmic quality of the harmonic change is influenced by a number of factors, often of no little subtlety and open to differences of opinion as to their values. . . ." We cannot object to a point of view so flexible although we sometimes find in his analyses more harmonies designated than seem necessary (in his example 78 he specifies I-II-I where the supertonic II may readily be considered decoration between the tonics).

I have no method to suggest which will give results that cannot be challenged, but I will say that the arrow-progressions in conjugations as discussed earlier are quite important throughout most of the nineteenth century and to some extent even in the present day. The first conjugation is used a very great deal, and chromatic effects are usually associated with this conjugation. I have just memorized and then analyzed Schumann's *Davidsbündlertänze* and the Brahms *Waltzes,* Op. 39; the progressions ii-V-I recur many times, though often in varying tonalities. Sometimes the entire circle I-IV-vii°-iii-vi-ii-V-I is found. Augmented sixths and Neapolitan effects abound. So we may watch for the shift from ii to V, etc., in the harmonic rhythm.

However, problems of harmonic rhythm cannot be separated from problems of structure, and these are related to melodic inflection. These facts were understood by Schenker, whose *Schichten* or layers were arranged from foreground to background in the music so that the *Ur-linie* or scale-wise sections of important notes in the melody coincide with large formal divisions even as extensive as:

(118)

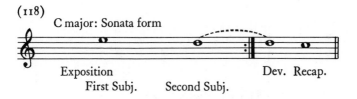

Each individual must decide, as he analyzes, on artistic premises, the rate of harmonic change in any particular composition, selecting what for him is an efficient way of thinking. Some persons can include more decoration than others and may be able to increase their musicianship until they arrive at something approaching Mozart's ability to hear all the notes of his composition at once. In practice it is wise to relegate as much to melodic decoration as possible.

When we come to Debussy and the impressionists, it is the use of anti-arrow or regressive movement which probably provoked the criticism that this music was lacking in harmonic function. It did not set the king-tonic on the throne supported on the right and left by the two dominants as before. The music seems in the passive voice even in its smaller minutiae:

The beginning of Debussy's *Reflets dans l'eau*

(119)

Double Ped. Pt. I   IV   iii   ii $\frac{4}{3}$

As long as we can do so with any satisfaction or benefit to ourselves, we should continue to use the harmonic experience and the techniques derived from analysis of older music. These represent the musical processes of thought in former generations; they continue to some extent in our own time. I remember that when I was memorizing the *Sechs kleine Klavierstücke* of Schönberg's Opus 19, the old techniques were still very useful. If you can refer to the music (Universal Edition), the following brief explanation of all the notes in number two of the set will illustrate the continued use of older terminology:

This piece is definitely in the key of G major as it begins with repetitions of the major third g′-b′; in measure two we have the leading-tone f♯′ and in measure three e′♭, a and c′ completing the diminished seventh of g minor. (Schönberg spells the e♭ as d♯ but, since he has stated that he is indifferent to the spelling of pitches and since he writes e♭ in the fourth measure, I call it e♭ to complete the diminished seventh of the key.) The third measure also contains, after this diminished seventh-outline, an a♭, the Neapolitan neighbor of G, and the fourth measure imitates in the same torculus-shape with a different third, c², and e²♭, borrowed from g-minor.

The fifth measure begins with the first vertical combination of any real complexity, consisting of the attendant chord f²♯-a²♯-e³ (spelled all in flats) in the right hand. In the left hand there is an echo of the c²-e²♭ figure from measure three. Thus we have an illustration of two harmonies used simultaneously, the result of an echo similar to that of the "horns" in Beethoven's *Lebewohl* from Op. 81. The only other notes in measure five form the third f♯-a♯ as auxiliary to the persistent g′-b′ although Schönberg places them in the lower octave in accordance with his disjunct style.

Teaching Music Theory

Measure six opens with three thirds: the Neapolitan, the second dominant, and the subdominant borrowed from g minor. The second complicated vertical combination completes this measure. It consists of b-d′, which resolves the three chromatic thirds just mentioned into G major, and in addition the same diminished chord on the leading-tone which we had in measures two and three, this time spelled by Schönberg F♯-B♯-d♯ instead of F♯-c-e♭, and further complicated by the addition of the low leading-tone f♮. Bach and many other composers have used this combination of low and raised leading tones in contrapuntal combination. Here the effect is used for its own sake. In this second complicated chord we again see an attendant effect coinciding with the resolution of a series of thirds.

There remain only three measures in this simple piece. The thirds g′-b′ continue in the right hand, and four thirds in the left hand alternate rhythmically, descending and passing: f-a, e♭-g, d♭-f and c-e, or, respectively, low leading-tone, VI of parallel minor, Neapolitan above the subdominant, and subdominant. After the four descending thirds, g′-b′ is heard for the last time, and then above we hear e♭², f♯², b♭² and d³. This involves what I call multiple leading-tones that do not resolve. The d³ completes the tonic triad with the g′-b′ which still sounds. For the third time Schönberg has used a peculiar spelling for an attendant chord: f♯-a♯-e♭; this time it is logical, for each note is a half-step from the G triad.

As in some modern plays, the curtain goes down on this piece with the audience forced to supply the resolution or to leave the situation unsolved; however, the resolution in this case is so natural and easy to imagine that it seems strange that it did not seem obvious to Hugo Leichtentritt, who speaks of E minor or B major as possible tonalities (*Musical Form,* page 445). Number three of Schönberg's Opus 19 also cadences with an unresolved dissonance: the augmented sixth inside the octave of the third (E♭-c♯) going to B♭-d (plus the added sixth and seventh). For the cadences of numbers one and five, which resolve one dissonance to another using multiple leading-tones, see later illustrations.

In music that may be said to possess a tonal center but not the usual progressions which in the past surrounded that center like the points of a compass, there are ways in which such a center may be emphasized or established. This is often done by the convergence of melodic lines, reminding us of the renewed emphasis upon counterpoint. The unison and the octave, preferably the perfect octave without triadic content, are very important as goals approached by

contrary motion. Either contract- (120)
ing toward a unison or expand-
ing toward an octave points up
this emphasis even if the final
unison or octave is not stated:

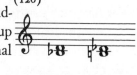

In this case C is pointed to. Sometimes the old dominant proceeds (usually in contrary motion) by extremely dissonant and seemingly illogical progressions
to the new tonal center, but more often used is the
modern dominant equidistant from the extremes of
the octave (to be discussed later). Octave skips in the
melody are also used to emphasize the tonal center;
and the device of the sequence, because it sets off as important the point of departure and the point of arrival,
is still effective, regardless of the material used.

Thus, logic and the logical sequence of movement
toward a point are still powerful. Mother nature has
not abdicated. It is true that many modern composers say they are merely exploring the upper
reaches of acoustical overtones, which are infinite
in number. However, the fundamental importance
of the lower partials cannot be ignored. Note how
effectively Aaron Copland has used structures of perfect fifths in his *Piano Fantasy* (1957). At important
points in that work he repeats the second overtone
of the fifth in a series which covers almost the
entire range of the instrument:

Harmony in the Twentieth Century

(121)

Aaron Copland, *Piano Fantasy,* mm. 837-852

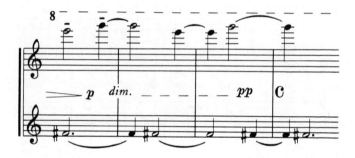

The composer uses this structure of perfect fifths (created by the use of the piano pedal) as a foil for his more dissonant series, the tone row on which the composition is based (this begins in our illustration in the bass of the sixth measure).

On the other hand, modern music gives increased importance to the semitone as an electrical discharge over the smallest gap in the tempered scale. This was early seen in the resolutions of augmented sixths but it finds a great extension in the appearance of multiple leading-tones and in its use for maximum tension — seen in the minor seconds, major sevenths or minor ninths in almost every chord of some scores.

While there are few sweeping generalizations which I can present on the subject of the harmony of the twentieth century, I would like to remind the reader of certain ideas in the earlier chapters which already point toward a wider use. It was stated that any two harmonies in the index of a given note go well together and that the entire index may be arranged in any order. In the music of the present day we find that this statement can be extended to include the connection of any chord of the original index with any chord chosen from indices on adjacent notes one-half step or one whole step above or below the original index. This is but another way of saying that all appoggiaturas have become members of harmonies and that any chord from the index of an appoggiatura can be associated with any chord of the index to which the original chord (adjacent to the appoggiatura) belongs.

(122)

For some time it has been recognized that there may be a telescoping of progressions, for instance, the resolution of an augmented-sixth chord appearing at the same time as the augmented chord. Dominant and tonic have long been vertically associated. As a natural consequence of the chromatic generalization of Major-hyphen-minor in Chapter XI we now have many illustrations of major-plus-minor in Hindemith and others: the octave filled with perfect fifth and both major and minor thirds at once (Hindemith's second *Piano Sonata,* third movement, measure 18, is a good illustration). We need to remember that the Neapolitan effect may occur as a slip-chord both above and below a triad. The following is an early illustration of the approach from below:

(123)

Wagner, *Tristan and Isolde,* Act I, Scene II, Measures 24-26

Isolde: Tod - ge - weih - tes Haupt

(124)

In the twentieth century they may also occur together:

Not only may any two chords from an index follow each other, they may occur simultaneously:

(125)

R. Strauss, *Salome,* Fourth Scene, Measures 462-3

er soll schwei - - gen

(126)

Puccini, *Turandot,* Act I, meas. 11

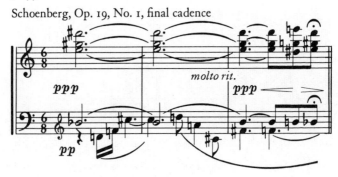

(e♯ - f♮)

What might be called multiple leading-tones may be used. They often occur in Schönberg's final cadences.

(127)

Schoenberg, Op. 19, No. 1, final cadence

(128)

Final cadence, Op. 19, No. 5

When you find five or six leading-tones before a final chord consisting of another five or six notes, you have a close resemblance to the Hauer tropes, in which a field of six notes is contrasted as subject with another field of the remaining notes as predicate. In Chapter VI of my book *Changing Forms in Modern Music,* I contrasted the forty-four tropes of J. M. Hauer with the Schönberg series, and stated that where the two halves of Hauer's tropes coincide with rhythmical units or recognizable structural combinations they have logical formal validity. Since that chapter was written many more analyses of the later works of Schönberg have been published; and most of these works are based upon tone-rows or

[225]

series of twice six notes. It would seem, therefore, that toward the end of his life Schönberg and his followers were consciously or unconsciously drawing nearer to the use of "tropes" since any choice of six notes followed by the other six as formal elements must of necessity be found in one of Hauer's forty-four (where the order of notes in the trope can be freely changed).

Other illustrations of all voices moving by half-steps can be found in such combinations as the following:

(129)

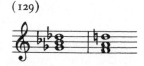

Wagner and others discovered these when combining triads freely.

Richard Strauss uses striking triadic successions such as Bb major, Ab major, and E major, in *Salome*. Such juxtapositions are even more effective since they do not contain an element of dissonance in themselves, that is, no seventh or ninth disturbs the solidity of each member. Each implies a "king" or a tonal entity, and they meet as kings rather than as underlings. However, such chord successions as the Gb-d above can also be referred to another generalization on chromatic harmony in Chapter XI, the one referring to "Major-hyphen-minor" or what might be called a twentieth century mode. Thus, in the illustration just given G♭ major equals g-flat minor, which en-harmonically is iii of D major, and that equals d minor; moreover, these chords belong to two adjacent indices. Triadic connections in which all voices move by half steps resemble the multiple leading-tones already discussed. They are also related to the movement of augmented sixth chords even if they do not contain that characteristic interval: the explosion of the c minor triad to E major second inversion is like the bottom three notes of one of the newer effects without the a-sharp (augmented sixth); and the C major triad to g-sharp minor first inversion is like the top three notes of a similar augmented sixth (a, c, e, f $\times$). If they were complete both would sound like explosive minor sevenths (alias "new" augmented sixths).

The renewed emphasis on melodic and contrapuntal, rather than purely harmonic, factors in the cadence has probably influenced the tonal centers chosen for important structural points in modern music. In my opinion there is a connection between the cadences so often used by Hindemith (in which the chords approach the tonal center by steps from each side, somewhat reminiscent of the "clausula vera") and the way in which the tonal centers of second subjects are related to the main tonality of the movement in his music. This relationship is rather obvious in the traditional sonata form, where the two parts of what was originally a binary form represent an extension of what might be called a half-cadence and a full cadence: I-V: V-I. The excursions after the start of the second half become so extensive that a complete return or recapitulation changes the entire form to a tripartite design; however, the key schemes of larger forms are related to the cadential formulas of different periods. For example, when the mediant relationships of the nineteenth century increased in importance as harmonic progressions they also assumed importance as tonal centers in sonata expositions. Both the leading tone and the sub-tonic or low leading tone have become important as roots of cadential structures in the twentieth century; they, and with them their pivotal counterparts a half-step and a whole step above the center, are used for second subjects as well. They assume an axis relationship in many Hindemith sonatas, as I have pointed out in Chapter IX of *Changing Forms in Modern Music*.

In the chapter on the dominant seventh it was suggested that anything may follow a dominant seventh as an irregular resolution. This is not far from the 20th century situation in which any dissonance can be followed by any other dissonance; as long as the succession contains dissonances the process can be continued. The term "relative tension" becomes applicable at this point, and such tables and diagrams as those in Hindemith's *Craft of Musical Composition* are indeed useful here. Do we now reach the position that the teaching of harmonic progression is no longer necessary? That would be absurdly defeatist. Choices are even more important when the liberty to make them is increased. There are many dangers which the student must avoid; even such an elementary suggestion as the statement that the subdominant has a tendency to undermine the tonal center if it is stressed too early in a composition is still relevant. Increase and decrease of tension must be carefully planned. The conjugations of roots are still valid regardless of the complexities of structures erected.

At present the lowest sound in any vertical structure is very important, the lower the sound (since the overtones have greater amplitude) the more important. If that lowest note is actually doubled in the octave its importance increases. (At this point one is in disagreement with Hindemith's method of finding his "roots." In the following chord:

(130)

Hindemith's root is e, the lower note of the "most important interval.") Rameau's structures of thirds still claim our attention provided we do not limit our vocabulary to chords of the ninth. Structures of perfect fourths with ambiguous roots enter tonality at points more and more distant from the bass the higher the structure.

(131)

Ex. 131 may be diatonic in F or B♭ but the addition of a fourth note, E♭, places it diatonically in B♭ or E♭, and six notes, C, F, B♭, E♭, A♭ and D♭, are diatonic in A♭ and D♭. Beyond that the lowest notes in a vertical series of perfect fourths become dissonant to the tonality of the upper notes. Conversely, when we take a diatonic thirteenth, as in ex. 132:

(132)

(133)

and re-arrange it as fourths, one of the fourths is not perfect (ex. 133):

In an earlier chapter it was stated that most of the prohibitions in conventional theory were based upon a dislike of organum and modal flavor. The twentieth century has rediscovered the middle ages; both in formal considerations and in harmony our century is more like the fourteenth century or earlier than it is like the eighteenth and nineteenth centuries. However, these effects are not used in their original context; it is always true in history that what appears new or old is something new-old or old-new. Originally, organum did not use the third of the triad, and since it was a melodic duplication of modal melodies most of the steps were whole ones. Chromatic slip-chord effects certainly do not remind anyone of the old organum:

(134)

Remembering that organum was predominantly diatonic in its use of whole-steps and that, in my opinion, the so-called rules against parallel fifths and octaves are attempts to eliminate the sound of organum in the music of what Piston calls the "period

of common-practice," we can understand why the
chromatic organum of parallel fifths in the resolution of the German augmented sixth chord to the
dominant triad:

(135)
Beethoven, *Sonata for Violoncello and Piano,* Op. 5, No. 1,
measures 127-9

was accepted and used by Beethoven, Chopin, and
nineteenth-century composers in general. To be sure
the timid author or teacher might still suggest that
one voice be resolved *before* the other to avoid these
parallel fifths, but the very fact that they are *chromatic*
removes any suggestion of the outmoded organum.
"Slip-chord" effects are now used for any type of harmonic structure, including the Debussy parallel ninths.
This parallel movement of any sound may be by
half-steps, whole steps or a combination of both. That
is, the movement in this combination may be within

the diatonic series of the major or minor mode, or in the pattern of any empirical scale manufactured by a composer. (These latter often do not permit a major or minor triad on the first note or a dominant seventh on the fifth.)

After a period in which modes other than the major and minor were largely overlooked there has been an important revival of their use in the present century — again, as in the case of organum, with a difference. It is true that the old modes never completely disappeared from music so that this statement, like many others in this book, is only a generalization. The romantic period discovered the strange beauty of modal flavor. Pan-diatonicism, or what might be called in terms of the piano keyboard "white-note impressionism," may be built upon the modal scales, using progressions of sevenths and other dissonant structures.

(136)

Milhaud: *Sonata* (1916), measures 22-23

In this style cadences may occur on unexpected triads
or on perfect fifths without a third present.

If there is a "dominant" in some music today it is
probably the augmented fourth or the diminished
fifth, half way between the two tonics. I believe this

fact was first demonstrated by Eaglefield Hull in his *Modern Harmony* (Augener Ltd., London). The new dominant and the old dominant (the second upper partial in terms of acoustical laws) alternate in such transitional styles as that of Scriabin's fifth sonata (mm. 304-327) and R. Strauss's *Don Quixote* (A flat to D, mm. 7-12). This modern dominant is the fifth note of the Locrian mode which, though it was not used in traditional modal practice, is implied in works by Debussy and others.

Just as the old dominant was the key choice at important formal divisions, so the modern dominant may be found in similar situations. The middle movement of Prokofieff's fifth piano sonata is in G♭, the first and last movements in C. Here is the same relationship of the tritone b-f in Strauss's *Salome:*

(137)

R. Strauss, *Salome,* Third Scene, measures 596-7

[235]

ver - - flucht

The example above is interesting because the modern dominant is used in the minor mode less frequently than in major. In the major mode we can see the relation of the modern dominant seventh to the index as in ex. 138. The seventh of the modern dominant chord is the third of the tonic.

(138)

It is also related to the idea of multiple leading-tones or movement by half or whole steps alone:

Bartok, No. 13 of 14 *Bagatellen,* Op. 6.

(139)

[236]

Only "modern dominants" or tritones are found in the whole-tone scale; and the same distance appears as a favorite basis for the transposition of tone-rows in 12-tone music (cf. Schönberg's *Suite fur Klavier,* Op. 25).

When it was stated that anything may be used as filler in augmented sixth chords and inside the octave of their resolution, we generalized many effects not treated in conventional texts, although these unusual effects were in use before the end of the nineteenth century. The whole-tone scale (any combination of which, even the complete scale vertically, forms a chord) is often used now for augmented-sixth fillers.

The French augmented sixth is a partial whole-tone scale; in its most usual location in C major it is spelled ab, c, d, f♯ with only the notes bb and e being omitted. Since any augmented sixth (diminished third) is also a whole step, the French augmented sixth explodes to two octaves (cf. Chapter XI); and when the entire whole-tone scale is used as a filler for augmented sixth effects it explodes to six different octaves, these octaves representing the other whole-tone scale. The chord and its possible resolutions contain all twelve notes. It is no wonder that a whole-tone chord may be followed by any chord or tonality.

(140)

octaves of resolution

(consider as a chord)

Such a complicated chord as a dominant thirteenth with augmented fifth and augmented eleventh is really an augmented sixth effect containing the whole-tone scale:

(141)

Equals

The newer augmented sixth effects account for much that has puzzled theorists. I have seen many explanations for the opening of Wagner's *Prelude* to *Tristan,* but the simplest is that it presents an augmented sixth (with the sound of a half-diminished seventh chord) inside the dominant octave (E) of the key of A minor, which key forms the background of the *Prelude* though its full cadence is not completed at the end.

(142)

The half-diminished sound as an augmented sixth inside the mediant octave is found in Strauss's *Till Eulenspiegel* (21 measures before the end):

(143)

Among the many new combinations with the augmented sixth structure, we find the sound of a Major ninth added to that of a minor seventh. It is usually written as a double-augmented octave (ex. 144):

(144)

(145)

Another possibility sounds like the last inversion of a dominant ninth but explodes like an augmented sixth (ex. 145):

When all is said about freedom of harmonic interplay, we must return to the fundamental problem of unity and variety, or the creation of a *Mikrokosmos*

[239]

in every composition. Beyond the "correct" in elementary progressions is the more and more beautiful. We must not lose our regard for the simple. As Edna St. Vincent Millay says in her sonnet on form:

> I will put chaos into fourteen lines
> And keep him there ...
> ... He is nothing more nor less
> Than something simple not yet understood;
> I shall not even force him to confess;
> Or answer. I will only make him good.

When a student presents the following during the first weeks of a freshman course, we should not discard it at once because of its apparent lack of knowledge of good part-writing:

(146)

Harmony in the Twentieth Century

This offers an opportunity to discuss organum as it was practiced in the tenth century and to contrast it with a style based upon historical precedent though very distantly related to it. In some respects the lot of the teacher of harmony, to paraphrase Gilbert and Sullivan, is not a happy one. He must continually defend that paradox — a changing standard! His best students are those who refuse to believe and obey him and he must rejoice in their disobedience and unbelief. Yet he must insist upon much of the old routine, using the well-worn arguments: "only he who knows the law thoroughly knows when to disobey it," or "before we permit you to throw paint at a canvas you must prove that you can draw something that looks like a human being," or "Who would like to play tennis with no lines on the court!", etc. The truth is that the artist like the saint is above law. To the extent that the student is a younger artist with at least a flickering inner light of musical instinct to guide him, this is true of him as well. Carlyle said, "Produce! Were it but the pitifulest infinitesimal fraction of a product, produce it in God's name!" (*Sartor Resartus,* Chapter 7).

This book has set down some of the writer's experience in teaching undergraduates and in teaching harmony teachers. I believe that there are benefits to be derived from disciplines and even from routines in education; we must not be afraid of using the mind and memory. There are transfers from one discipline to another in education and if such transfers do not occur the teaching is at fault. At the same time I recognize the dangers in routine, especially routine which touches the artistic process; for the artistically creative mind must take the initiative in every one of its steps in the future, acting from inner compulsion. The sooner a teacher becomes unnecessary, the better; he should be constantly striving to find himself out of a job.

We need to remember that generalizations regarding harmonic practice are based on historical procedures and as such are connected with the social-political attitudes of the past. We need to teach with an historical perspective, which includes the tenth and twentieth centuries as well as the eighteenth and nineteenth, realizing that music is a living language still in process of change. Generalizations are no substitute for a thorough acquaintance with the details of technique. They are an end result of experience, not a beginning, and they depend upon the integration in music of ear, eye and finger. We lose the infinite variety of living art when we theorize or generalize; but the student should take generalizations in his stride and not be subjugated by them. The usual or normal becomes then a kind of second nature for him and when he does the exceptional and original he will be sure of himself; freedom in the use of an infinite variety of harmonies comes from mastery achieved through practice of generalized procedures.

CHAPTER XIII

Teaching Other Theoretical Subjects

W E have come to the end of what I wanted
to say about the teaching of fundamental musicianship, rhythm, melody and harmony, arriving in
Chapter XII at a point far removed from the simple
propositions with which we began. Frequent references have been made to the contrapuntal or horizontal aspects of harmony;* however, separate studies
of counterpoint, canon and fugue deserve in each case
a larger book than this one if they are to be thor-

*I have intentionally stopped short of a discussion of teaching methods
for serial music. There are a number of good references listed in the next
chapter.

oughly discussed. There is also a question of where the line is to be drawn between the so-called theoretical subjects and the historical-musicological subjects. Where should we classify orchestration, analysis of form, and courses often called Introduction to Music, popularly known as "Appreciation" of the art?

A few convictions regarding the teaching of these subjects I will state here; the experienced teacher may or may not agree. Beginning with the last-named topic, I believe the best approach for the general listener is an introduction to the forms of music through the ear. This seems like an absurdly simple statement to make; let us see what it implies. The student who is majoring in another field is not likely to carry musical scores to concerts; he may not be able to read music from the printed page. When time is limited, as it usually is, in this introductory course, the so-called visual aids waste time and in fact add something which distracts the ear. I could almost wish that all the students in such a course were temporarily sightless when listening to music so that they might concentrate upon contours and content that the musical language presents as it speaks to them. Then I would keep out of the classroom, where time is so precious, practically all material which can be gained by students from the reading of books. Reading of this sort may be made a requirement of the course, but the classroom should be saved for what cannot be gotten from books. This does not mean that the work with the class should avoid references to historical styles. These are very important in their relation to the forms which are presented, and, of course, an understanding of style is necessary for true comprehension. The order in which music is presented should be from the more simple to the more complex, and this, at least from the standpoint of the student, is not necessarily an historical order. However, I have not found a complete reversal of the historical order entirely satisfactory because of the complexity of much of our music today. In my experience, beginning with the music of Haydn and Mozart, choosing their simplest and most nearly regular compositions, such as variation movements, is best. From that point we may proceed in two directions: first forward to the nineteenth century, and then back to earlier music, after which the twentieth century claims attention. This juxtaposition brings out the fact that our century is in some respects more like the fifteenth than the eighteenth.

For the future professional musician a thorough course in formal analysis should be undertaken. In this course both eye and ear should be used to the utmost degree; also, the more the student is able to have first-hand acquaintance with the music, the better. The use of recordings should be discouraged when the student is able to read from score, particularly when the music was originally written for performance at a keyboard; one hopes that his inner ear will come to his rescue when fingers falter. Here the didactic purpose is quite different from that of the introductory course above. Detailed analysis of form, done both microscopically and macroscopically, is the objective here. To be sure, the teacher may occasionally wish to test even the advanced student regarding his ability to perceive formal details of a composition through the ear; the approach should not be exclusively visual or entirely aural.

The method of a laboratory is best at this advanced level. Students should be constantly faced with decisions concerning music for which they have no definite expectations or categories. Conventional formal divisions and the various methods of formal analysis should be reviewed as rapidly as possible, and then the students should be given a body of material in which any one of a dozen possibilities may prove to be correct. The use of miscellaneous unknowns is much better than the assignment, for analysis, of examples of the same formal type, leaving all other types aside for the moment. The forms themselves are so often interrelated that at least a superficial knowledge of all of them may be necessary before analysis of any individual composition may be undertaken. In other words, after the study of conventional nomenclature and the history of forms, the student should be given music in which he has little expectation in advance as to what he may find in the material. This will be the situation when he graduates from the classroom. For help in his practical work of memorizing or conducting new music, he should early cultivate the habit of conscious or unconscious analysis. Even in the collections so often used for the primary forms, such as Schumann's *Album für die Jugend,* Mendelssohn's *Songs without Words,* or Chopin's *Preludes,* he will find great variety and many sub-species.

The student should understand that two or more differing opinions concerning the same composition may be defended appropriately and logically. It is the skill shown in defense of his own analysis, done with some knowledge of the history of and literature on the subject, which is important. There is possibility of confusion among the several systems of terminology in this field, and I have heard many pleas for standardization voiced when teachers of music convene. I have never listened to them very sympathetically because I believe that any teacher should be familiar with all methods of analysis that have been used in the past, and the important thing for teacher and student is to be consistent both in method and in the use of the terminology which he chooses. There are many disagreements about the labels placed upon details of form by recognized authorities. They run all the way from two opposing analyses of *The Bluebells of Scotland* (Ebenezer Prout calling it binary and Stewart Macpherson labelling it ternary) to the glib acceptance of Strauss's *Till Eulenspiegel* as a rondo on the basis of the composer's reference in his subtitle (which may have been written with tongue in cheek a la *Till*), even though many careful analysts, at least in the German literature on this piece, point to it as being in sonata form.

A teacher may not wish to adopt the methods and results of past analysis, but he should be familiar with them, particularly with the main approaches of Hugo Riemann, Alfred Lorenz, Heinrich Schenker and Georg Eduard Conus (unfortunately the writings of Conus, with their architectural approach, are available only in Russian). Jacques Chailley, Helmut Federhofer and Felix Salzer follow Schenker; Ilmari Krohn's work is based partly upon Riemann; Paul Egert, Herman Grabner, Alfred Orel and Heinz Röttger use in part the methods of Lorenz. There is at least partial validity in all the main approaches. Good books in English are those by Stewart Macpherson and Hugo Leichtentritt. It is the research

Teaching Other Theoretical Subjects

method of the laboratory which has a special appeal for the more brilliant students who wish to become intelligent musicians. There is much more to be done, especially in the field of contemporary music.

The study of orchestration, like that of any other aspect of music, belongs both in the division of history and in that of theory. There are many different ideas or ideals for the sound of music today, as well as for its vocabulary or its formal structure. We find the idea of blended sound at the base of much of orchestral thinking in the nineteenth century, and Rimsky-Korsakoff's two volumes clearly state when he succeeded in achieving a good blend and when he did not. At the mid-twentieth century the ideal is just the opposite. Vivid and independent lines of orchestral color, clear-cut and often austere ensembles are desired by most composers. Basic, of course, is a knowledge of what the instruments can do, and the more this knowledge comes from first-hand acquaintance, the better. The time is long past when Brahms and Bruckner can be criticized for their individual orchestral dress. Each composer will have his own individuality in this respect as in all the other elements of his style. In addition to Rimsky-Korsakoff, other composers have written books on orchestration, each presenting to some extent his personal preferences: Berlioz, Widor, Piston, Cecil Forsyth,

Teaching Music Theory

Kent Kennan and Bernard Rogers. Two books unique in their emphases are those of Joseph Frederick Wagner and Gardner Read. Wagner's practical handbook contains extensive reference charts of keyboard idioms and patterns translated into orchestral score; Read's *Thesaurus of Orchestral Devices* cites the exact locations where thousands of instrumental effects may be found — for instance, the use of extreme or extended ranges in the woodwinds, effects which are so characteristic of our century. Any book on orchestration should be read as the expression of one man's opinion, representing the perspectives of his period.

There are also many kinds of counterpoint. Usually the list begins with the sixteenth century, where it is associated with the style of Palestrina; but why begin there! Would it not be logical to begin with much earlier styles? Palestrina's counterpoint is already harmonic from our point of view. The more study any period receives, the further back the origins of certain processes of thought seem to reach. Not only is the word "never" a dangerous word in theoretical artistic disciplines; the word "first" can only be used with great caution after long study. Ideally, a student might recapitulate the history of music, as Vincent d'Indy urged in his *Cours de composition musicale,* and write contrapuntally in all styles in succession, hoping in this fashion to know what the next step today should be. It would be presumptuous to attempt to discuss in detail here the various types of counterpoint. J. S. Bach's polyphony is not the same as that in his sons' fugues. The fugues in Schubert's *Mass in E♭* differ from those of Beethoven's last period. Wagner's counterpoint, as in *Die Meistersinger*, becomes a little more dissonant in Strauss's *Ein Heldenleben*. Again the rules of the game change in Hindemith's *Ludus tonalis* and in Schönberg's compositions. In Ernst Krenek's *Studies in Counterpoint* dissonances are normal and consonances abnormal. Kurth's term "linear counterpoint" is tautological but useful in describing a dissonant angular style which has almost returned in full circle to a point where counterpoint pays little or no attention to the harmonic verticals.

Unfortunately, a student's academic life may be too short to permit him to experiment in all these styles, and the teacher will need to decide where to lay the emphasis in the limited time at his disposal. Should some of his time be devoted to strict counterpoint in the five species if they are thought to form a theoretical foundation for the treatment of horizontal voices? While the results may be criticized as not representing the style of any actual musical period, the writing of contrapuntal exercises based on Fux or Cherubini and their many successors may have beneficial results. Even the writing of a number of different counterpoints to the same *cantus firmus* may bring the realization that beyond work merely correct there is more and more beautiful work. A. Tillman Merritt and Knud Jeppesen are better guides to good sixteenth-century style than Fux; however, the species still represent something like pure or idealized design, perhaps akin to mechanical drawing in the visual arts. Probably a student should have some practice in working within the species' limitations before he begins to throw his paint at the canvas, musically speaking.

The twentieth century has witnessed a revival of interest in contrapuntal style. With the weakening of harmonic claims, the importance of horizontal lines, singly and in combination, has increased. When I first began to study the use of twelve-note series in music approaching atonality, it seemed that only the contrapuntal methods of imitation, inversion, cancrizans, etc., used in invention, canon, and fugue, could secure validity for its forms. There is no doubt a special virtue in the fugal treatment of a tone-row; contrapuntal methods seem to justify any vertical combination, and this principle can be extended, as we have seen, to streams of chords as well as to single-line melodies. While I no longer believe that twelve-tone music is limited to these styles, they remain some of its most effective outlets. If all lines are melodically plausible, the feasibility of their vertical combination is usually guaranteed.

Bach certainly did not think of counterpoint and harmony as separate studies. In some curricula, counterpoint has been taught before courses in harmony; there are also ingenious schemes which interlock the two subjects — first species counterpoint and then triadic harmony, second species counterpoint and then harmony with chords of the seventh, and so on. Edward C. Bairstow has a text based upon this order. The study of music suffers from over-departmentalization. Actually counterpoint and harmony are interrelated; attention should be directed in harmony to individual melodic lines, and, in counterpoint, to harmonic implications.

As has often been said, fugue is a style and not a form, in any precise sense of the word. While many fugues may be analyzed as tripartite forms, there are almost as many that may be appropriately considered binary. Siegmund Levarie, using the nomenclature of Alfred Lorenz, finds five different forms in the first book of Bach's *Wohltemperiertes Clavier;* and, of course, each of the forty-eight is an individual development within the style. If we use the outline of what has been called the school-fugue, we should be careful not to give the impression that many great

[255]

fugues follow that outline. The freedom of the cur-
sive flow of exposition, episodes and re-expositions
must be preserved. It has also seemed to me that
it is not quite reasonable to ask a student to write
a lengthy fugue upon a subject which you, as teacher,
give to him, one possibly taken from a textbook
or from a fugue by a great composer. I admit that
the writing of a good fugue subject is not a simple
assignment by any means; but if you ask for a considerable number of original subjects from students,
some of the results will probably have possibilities
and may be modified by criticism and alteration into
decent subjects. In the meantime the student is learning something about the real nature of a fugue and
the strength of its personality, as heard in the subject itself, even before the fugal treatment begins. I
believe that students learn by trying, and that they
enjoy trying and learning more if they know that
the results will be all their own. Of course, there
are many great fugues upon derived subjects, such
as those upon the name of Bach; still, we should
permit the student to choose or create his own subjects.

In the chapter on fugue in *Changing Forms
in Modern Music,* I point out that the use of the
supertonic for the third entry, as well as the presence of tonalities other than tonic and dominant

for entrances of subject and answer in the exposition of modern fugues, has broken down the distinctions normally present in that form, although the responsory effect continues. Just as the modern sonata may be seen as all development, or the disappearance of the common triad may seem to cause a loss of clarity in other forms, the advisability of this procedure may be questioned. The exposition no longer presents an architecture of upright verticals, but is more like a cubistic or expressionistic stage-setting, supported only by the imagination of the designer. The student will do well to delay such experiments until he is thoroughly familiar with fugal construction.

Perhaps we may consider the course which is given the title "Composition" as the capstone of the theory curriculum which the student has been following; however, I am inclined to believe that the best thing about that item in the course catalogue is that it secures for the capable student some time in his crowded schedule for writing. I doubt if any of the books on the subject are of much help; the best teachers of these courses place the burden of production upon the student, reserving comments and suggestions until they see what the student has written. Routine formulas seem out of place here. Even a prescribed hierarchy of forms in which to compose, from monoform to sonata form or from a round to a fugue, is not always advisable. Fortunately some academic institutions now realize that they should give the most talented members of their junior and senior classes the opportunity to work at their own speed, and to a considerable extent without detailed direction, in research projects and composition in the arts as well as in literature. This is sometimes given the label "Independent Study" or "Honors Project," and there may be the prerequisite of a high grade-average for such study, possibly restricted to a maximum of six or eight hours in the normal year of 30 to 32 hours of credit. Fortunate also is the situation where such a label removes these hours from the maximum which may be taken in any one department, where, in other words, such research in the sciences or in creative writing is not charged to a specific department. Work is encouraged through a liberal allowance of time, so necessary for this type of study, which cannot be judged by the completion of routine assignments from week to week. It is the total product at the end which receives the credit and the grade required by most academic systems.

Stanley Kunitz, in *Harper's Magazine* of October, 1959, speaks in the guise of a poet advising the young man who wants to write. If you change the word writer to composer and substitute musical for literary references, his remarks are just as pertinent in the problem of teaching composition:

[258]

Teaching Other Theoretical Subjects

A writer is either experimental or dead. Most of the writers, however, who insist on labeling themselves as 'experimental' are simply not sure of themselves. Each literary generation requires the existence of an *avant-garde*, not because the latter are more advanced than the writers of reputation, or superior to them, but because the prevailing style of a period needs always to be resisted if it is not to grow lax, needs always to be modified to keep it supple. Sometimes the nature of the resistance is in effect a backward look, but to a different set of ancestors from those venerated by the mandarins. This happens *not* to be a time of great innovation in poetic technique: it is rather a period in which the technical gains of past decades, particularly the 'twenties, are being tested and consolidated.

Creative writing cannot be taught. It is better to permit the advanced student to decide what he wants to write and how he writes. The content of the course is the students' work. Too often the beginning teacher of composition assigns a certain form, perhaps that of a theme and variations, without realizing that only the very best composers, and these composers only in fullest maturity toward the end of their lives, have written great works in this very difficult form. As Archibald MacLeish says concerning similar courses in English composition, "It is the student who knows, or should, and the teacher who learns or tries to." The teacher must judge only how well the student expresses his own ideas; he must not impose ideas and forms from above. If the approach throughout the musical curriculum has emphasized creativity, the student will not be at a loss for something to say when, near the end of his student career, he is given the liberty and the necessary time to express himself. However, the opportunity should be both elective and selective; both the student and the teacher should agree that the time will be well spent; and the option should be offered only to those who will make good use of it

CHAPTER XIV

Choice of Textbook

I T is my hope that this chapter may serve not only as an introduction to the more extended bibliography at the end of the volume but also as an attempt to help the beginning teacher who is worried over choosing a text.

I might begin by saying that any text may be used. What the teacher brings to the text in his background, gained from experience and from the reading of many books, is more important than the particular book chosen. A good teacher can use any text, or no text, as a point of departure. There are merits and demerits in all texts and the perfect book for use in the classroom has not been written. Because the good teacher can see objections to any one text, some excellent teachers prefer to use none; however, this is not the solution which I would recommend. Almost any text saves time and adds to the efficiency of the course, provided it is not used slavishly. Assignments in a text may be stated with little loss of time, or a syllabus may contain outlined assignments for a semester in advance. I have observed some teachers who seem to be dictating their own textbook to their students, sentence by sentence. If they have unique theories not yet available in print, this may be necessary on occasion; however, to do so with material that is the common property of almost any text is a sheer waste of time.

Again, the teacher or the author of a text who feels that he must invent and use an entirely different vocabulary and nomenclature for his ideas should think a long time before doing so. I present no apologies and need no justification for using figured bass or the symbols of *basso continuo*. These have historical validity. A musician needs to know how to realize such a continuo when he finds it in scores or manuscripts, although it is true that his professional life as a performer does not depend upon his facility in using these figures at the keyboard as it once did for the harpsichordist or organist.

Choice of Textbook

The reader will discover what I like or dislike in the comments which follow in connection with various texts. A few more general remarks may be made first. While I have no objection to the appearance of figured basses in a text since they have a certain historical pertinence, there is no such thing as a figured soprano either in history or in fact. Figured-bass symbols under soprano melodies serve, in my opinion, no useful purpose unless a Roman numeral accompanies them, in which case we no longer have a figured soprano but a figured bass. Figured basses offer additional illustrations of the material under discussion together with some practice in realization, but figured sopranos are a nuisance, of neither historical nor practical value. They are merely a guessing-game in which the student tries to find out what the author has in mind; moreover, if the conjugations discussed in this book have been mastered, the choice of harmonies for a given soprano can be left to the student.

For the sake of association in ear training I prefer a text in which different sounds have different symbols; i.e., instead of large Roman numerals for every degree of the scale, the symbols should represent the triads found on the degrees of the major and harmonic minor scales: I, ii, iii, etc. in major or i, ii°, III, etc., in minor. These will also serve for the diatonic sevenths, with the figure seven as exponent. To be sure, with ninths and larger structures additional figures and accidentals may be necessary; and of course in pure minor and in the modes, the numerals should agree with the triadic structure in each case); i.e., for pure minor (Aeolian mode): i, ii°, III, iv, v, VI, VII, i, and so forth.

Before I begin a discussion of specific texts I would like to mention again an author whose influence has been rather widespread and beneficial. I refer to Heinrich Schenker. Extremely conservative in his point of view (always insisting upon *Urlinie* or analyses conditioned by tonality), he has at the same time widened our idea of the bounds of tonality. In his final analysis, the influence of the tonic chord covers an entire composition. It is true that a single harmony, even in superficial analysis, covers more space in a composition than had been realized in most theories. As opposition to mechanical totaling of columns of notes indiscriminately called chords, Schenker's methods have been very beneficial for there are probably fewer chords in all music than most theorists have catalogued. His disciple, Felix Salzer, in the two volumes of *Structural Hearing* presents an important interpretation, and William J. Mitchell in his *Elementary Harmony* acknowledges his indebtedness. I would urge any teacher of theory to become better acquainted with Schenker's ideas although they can be reduced to absurdity if carried to excess. Too much analysis may take time which should be given to creative synthesis; however, when you analyze for memorization and understanding, the fewer chords you need to remember, the better.

Mr. Frank W. Hill, of Iowa State Teachers College, made a study of texts in use in 1939, and followed this by another questionnaire in 1947. It would be interesting to repeat his enquiries today. In 1939 the text most widely used was by Wedge. In 1947 Walter Piston's *Harmony* was at the head of the list. This book by Piston has some unique assignments, in an attempt to avoid giving the student either bass or soprano melodies. They read as a series of directions for modulating to certain keys, suggesting certain harmonies but leaving the details entirely to the student. However, the use of undifferentiated Roman numerals as symbols is, in my opinion, unfortunate from the standpoint of ear-training by constant association. The most important new emphasis in Piston's text is his discussion of harmonic rhythm; i.e., the rhythm of changes in harmony, different from that of any feature or voice represented in the music itself. The rate of change is important; so is the location of the accent produced by the change. Although, so far as I know, Piston was not directly influenced by Schenker's theories, he does increase the span of each harmony considerably.

Allen McHose of the Eastman School of Music presents in his book, *The Contrapuntal Harmonic Technique of the 18th Century* (1947), the results of analysis, done with the help of graduate students, of the progressions in Bach's chorales. In this connection we face at once the difficult question: "When is a chord a chord?" One has only to refer to Schenker or Piston to see how involved this question can become. However, the results as set forth by McHose in a table of chord relationships (page 13) agree with the order of progression and regression which I set up in three conjugations ("Harmony Reviewed," *Music Educators Journal,* March, 1944). This is to be expected. If any tabulation has validity, the findings secured through analysis should be approximately the same regardless of the composer or the work selected, at least for the period of common practice. For the sake of clarity I prefer the three conjugations as opposed to one table which includes all progressions and regressions.

Donald Tweedy is another writer whose text of harmony is based upon Bach's procedures. The book (*Manual of Harmonic Technique Based on the Practice of J. S. Bach*) deserves to be better known.

There was a slight increase in its use between 1939 and 1947 according to Hill's reports.

Frank Gannet in *Bach's Harmonic Progressions* presents a thousand examples, drawn from Bach's *371 Chorales,* of various harmonizations for the steps and skips of the major and minor scales, both ascending and descending. In other words, he shows us what harmonies Bach used when going from the first to the second note of the scale, from the first to the third, and so on. For the most part Gannet selects the notes as found in the soprano voice, but when they are infrequent or entirely absent in that voice he uses the other voices, most often the bass. From the Schenker point of view, the second notes of Gannet's intervals may really be passing notes.

The problem of choosing a text is most often raised by the teacher in elementary or secondary schools. There is no book which is entirely satisfactory, but I would recommend the reading of Ross Lee Finney's *The Game of Harmony* to anyone who wishes to introduce harmony in the elementary grades. He has a whimsical way of stating his ideas. The books by Angela Diller are also excellent. Osborne McConathy and his associates, Embs, Howes and Fouser, planned *An Approach to Harmony* with the secondary schools in mind. It has the virtue of not attempting to cover too much ground since it deals only with primary triads. However, the constant use of soprano patterns substitutes mechanical drill where broader guiding principles might be used. *Harmony Simplified* by Ralph L. Baldwin and Arthur F. A. Witte has the same objectives, but is inconsistent; it prohibits on one page what the authors present as a satisfactory illustration on the next (pp. 11-12). Also the authors state that IV to V^6 is to be avoided, when as a matter of fact this progression is frequently found with a skip of a diminished fifth in the bass. Alfred Hill's *Melody and Harmony* is not a text in the ordinary sense, but it illustrates how the succession of primary triads (I-IV-I-V; I-IV-I-V-I) may be used to harmonize many melodies and how this series may be expanded in the composition of a song.

Arthur Foote and Walter Spalding cooperated in the writing of their *Modern Harmony*. It is probable that the book was planned for a first-year college course since it presupposes a background in musicianship which the average student in a secondary school would not possess. Certain musical details are introduced before they are explained, and there is no attempt to pre-digest material for the student. In the hands of a good teacher the book may still be used. George W. Chadwick's *Harmony* (1897) went through fifty editions. In an appendix to the fiftieth edition (1922) there is an attempt to bring the text up to date. Like the appendix of the Foote and Spalding text in its more recent editions, this is not entirely successful. J. Humphrey Anger's *A Treatise on Harmony,* in three volumes, presents a personal and peculiar nomenclature. Sixteen pages of figured bass symbols are given although the principles upon which these are based could have been condensed into one paragraph. One distinction which Anger makes, namely that there is a logical difference between the order of perfect fifth to diminished fifth and its reverse, diminished fifth to perfect fifth, should receive more general agreement. The latter seems to imply the sound of hidden fifths; thus Anger permits the former progression between any two voices but the latter order only in upper voices.

As for books to be used in sight-singing, the relative unfamiliarity of their contents is a virtue; also important is the care with which they are arranged in order of increasing difficulty. Since excerpts from actual compositions should be found in these books, this gradation is not always easy to secure because composers do not write with a demonstration of degrees of difficulty in mind. Complexities of rhythm may occur with simple relationships of pitch, and vice versa. A good book for this purpose is McHose and Tibbs' *Sight Singing Manual.*

In most institutions there is no separate course in harmonic analysis. This is understandable since a thorough course in harmony includes analysis as one method of procedure. However, if you wish to use a text in this field, nothing is better than the works of some composer noted for the variety of his harmony: the Chopin *Préludes* for mid-nineteenth century effects, for instance. Special textbooks have the advantage of placing in the students' hands excerpts from many different composers. There are three such books, by Cutter, Lehmann, and Piston. Of the three, Lehmann gives the greatest variety of material for the student to use in analysis. Piston's book analyzes in the text most of his illustrations and hence it might be considered merely an adjunct to his *Harmony*. If harmonic analysis is to be useful, the harmonic vocabulary should have been mastered, in theory at least, and then the student should be given a body of material to analyze in which he has little assurance that any particular harmonic effect will appear. The Lehmann book does list at the head of each chapter the special effect being considered, but there are so many other items usually present in any excerpt that in the hands of an expert teacher the music offers sufficient variety to be interesting. The ideas in both Cutter and Lehmann are somewhat old-fashioned, but the excerpts they present can be analyzed from a more modern standpoint in class.

The authors of certain harmony textbooks have realized all the exercises in their texts in four-part notation, and it is interesting to compare these realizations with the statements which the authors make in their texts. For each of three older texts: Prout, Heacox-Lehmann, and Foote-Spalding, *Keys* have been published with the exercises harmonized by the authors. In each there are instances in which the author does not obey his own rules or prescriptions.

Teachers of musical theory should know of the new *Journal of Music Theory,* several issues of which have now appeared under the editorship of David Kraehenbuehl. Although a number of the articles do not concern the immediate task of the classroom teacher, the reviews and letters from correspondents are interesting and some of the articles deal with practical problems.

In addition to texts intended for the classroom, important books written by composers in explanation of their styles or of their thinking concerning theoretical matters should be carefully read. Those written by contemporary composers are particularly important.

We are always fortunate when a composer takes the time to set down his theories for us. Paul Hindemith's *Unterweisung im Tonsatz* has been adequately translated into English as *The Craft of Musical Composition.* There are two volumes, the first of which may be considered his "Harmony" and the second, his "Counterpoint." In addition we have his excellent book on fundamental musicianship, *Elementary Training for Musicians,* to which I have already referred. This prepares the student for the present day in many of its exercises for eye, ear and keyboard.* The important feature of his main work is a method of evaluating all possible vertical combinations, differing in many ways from the Rameau structure of thirds. The tabular view of this reclassification is most important for any student. His discussion of the construction of periods shows an excellent application of these values for increasing tension in the middle and decreasing it at the ends of periods. The fact that his compositions in the main agree with his theories may account for his music's unmistakable punctuation. He sets a fine example, cogent in form, of the relation of theory to practice, although, as in so many cases, the statement of the theories followed much composition. However, for practical use in analyzing tension, there does not seem to be sufficient distinction in relative dissonance within Hindemith's classifications. For instance, both of the following chords are in III_2, a subdivision of his third group:

---

*Hindemith also wrote a text entitled *A Concentrated Course in Traditional Harmony,* which is just what its name implies. Although he states in the preface the urgent necessity of covering its field in as short a time as possible, he presents few, if any, specific methods to further that end.

(147)

but most listeners would say that there is a great
difference in the amount of dissonance in these two
combinations. Similarly, the following are both in
IV$_1$:

(148)

Some account should probably be taken of the relative number of whole steps and half steps in combinations. The first, under III$_2$ above, contains one
whole step and the second, one half-step. The first
chord quoted from IV$_1$ has one half-step and one
whole step (as ninth and seventh respectively), while
the second one contains two half-steps (minor seconds), plus another written as an augmented octave.
The tritone, which is the feature not present in III
but which all combinations in IV have in common,
does not seem to be a sufficient distinction even when
Hindemith's idea of inversion is used for subdivisions
of the numeral classifications. If all the elements of
relative dissonance are included, the Table will pre-

sent many more distinctions which should prove useful.

Another important discussion of Hindemith's methods, which is not found in his books, is in his preface* to his revision in 1948 of a song-cycle first published in 1923. Some of the songs are completely rewritten, some are changed but little, and one, not at all. The preface presents thorough discussion of the reasons for the changes. In it Hindemith also acknowledges his great interest in the use of certain tonalities for certain ideas and characters: B major for Mary, E major for Christ, C major for eternity, Eb major for purity, F major (located at a tritone from B major) for falsehood and shortsightedness, etc. This reminds one of that part of Alfred Lorenz's studies of Wagner's operas in which he believes that he has found similar considerations. It would be interesting to compare the two.

Arnold Schönberg's *Harmonielehre* has been translated into English but with important omissions. It is better to read the original German edition if possible. However, do not go to this work expecting to find lengthy discussions of harmonic progressions in an advanced idiom. Most of the book lays a solid foundation for present-day writings, and points forward in a suggestive way. Of even greater import-

---

Einleitende Bemerkungen zur neuen Fassung (1948) Das Marienleben.

ance is his *Structural Functions of Harmony,* with its chart of the regions of tonalities (page 20) showing the relationship of all other tonalities to C major. Again, you will look in vain for an introduction to his later styles since the illustrations from his own compositions are all taken from his early works, ending with his *Kammersymphonie.* His *Models for Beginners* also helps the teacher to realize that a most advanced composer still believes in the necessity of seeing that every student has a firm foundation in traditional harmony. If you wish to study the literature dealing with the use of twelve-tone series, I would suggest in addition to certain short essays of Schönberg, Rufer's *Composition with Twelve Notes* and Krenek's *Studies in Counterpoint.* What I have to say on this subject may be found in my book *Changing Forms in Modern Music,* and I shall not offer suggestions on this style here.

The French composer Messiaen stated some of his theories and related the sources of his inspirations in the two volumes of *Technique de mon langage musical,* now translated in English. His *Twenty Examples of Harmony* (in the style of a few important masters of the history of harmony from Monteverdi to Ravel") is also available. In the work of this composer many of the devices discussed earlier in this book are used. There is an emphasis upon melody in various complex strands, together with more use of oriental types, bird songs, etc. From the standpoint of form he utilizes additive fractions in devising freer and more complex melodic rhythms. In his *Danse de la fureur, pour les sept trompettes* one melodic measure consists of a dotted eighth, a quarter-note tied to a sixteenth, a half-note, and again a quarter tied to a sixteenth, followed by a dotted eighth-note.

Roger Sessions in his *Harmonic Practice* disclaims any attempt to present a theory of contemporary practices. Since most of the illustrations in the book are his own, however, and since a number of the exercises are realized by him in Appendix B, we have examples in the latter part of the book which are "pure Sessions." If you admire the author's compositions you should by all means secure the book if only for its last one hundred pages.

George F. McKay has a slender volume on the *Technique of Modern Harmony* which contains useful assignments and projects for class use. Koechlin and Karg-Elert, both composers of some importance, have lengthy treatises in French and German, respectively. A number of other books which deal with this century are listed in the bibliography. The definitive text is yet to be written. What composers have to say regarding theory is important, but most composers have said what they have to say in their music, and to that we must go for any real understanding of this century.

We should not hesitate to acquaint our students with the complexities of music in our day. Simplicity before complexity is worth little, but simplicity beyond or after complexity is worth all the effort that is necessary to secure it. It is worth everything for it means mastery and the freedom that comes with it.

CHAPTER XV

Assignments and Special Projects

I F our students are to arrive at the freedom which comes from mastery and the simplicity which is beyond complexity, we must not spare them the labor that goes with routine work in any language. We must adapt our assignments to the ability and needs of our students; yet a schedule must be set up and maintained. When projects that involve some degree of self expression are used, the teacher must guard against a situation in which non-musical courses, with more definite problems to be solved, engage all the students' attention. The harmony teacher who, using figured basses or sopranos to be harmonized, assigns "the next ten exercises" may be able to compete with the teacher of mathematics who assigns the next ten problems. That is probably one of the reasons why so many figured basses have persisted in our texts. But the teacher who asks for creative expression will have to insist upon deadlines being met although he knows that there is a great difference in the educational value of merely keeping students active with "busy-work" and that of artistic self-expression.

If we decide to try the way of freedom, how may we prevent the student's losing his way? The answer, it seems to me, is to give him freedom within certain enclosures, progressively larger, in which he may make his own choices. As soon as he proves his mastery within a given area, add more territory. With a figured bass the author of the text is choosing the harmonic successions. When melodies are assigned to be set, the melodies are not the student's own. We may urge him to sing the melodies, memorize them and try to make them his own; even then the harmonization may be far from what the author of the text had in mind. One unconventional chord choice, perfectly valid in itself, may set the exercise off in a direction which makes the rest of the expected harmonization almost impossible. In any case, one of the important aspects of composition, both melody and harmony coming together in a real creative act, is violated.

In addition, therefore, to the exercises in the typical textbook which you may have selected for your class, you should invent many other types of assignments that that will place more responsibility upon the shoulders of the students. After they have composed and improvised successively within each of the fields suggested in this book: with rhythm alone, with melody in rhythm over one perfect fifth as accompaniment, and so on, ask them to write musical sentences consisting entirely of progressions in the usual direction plus the shuttle-trains between tonic and dominant or between subdominant and tonic. The result will sound like the exercises of any text which is based upon the period 1600 to 1900. Then ask them to write a number of sentences containing only regressions or anti-arrow movement. These will obviously sound quite different: pre-1600 or post-1900, i.e., more like Palestrina or Debussy, for instance. Then suggest a judicious mixture of both directions in a proportion that approximates eight or nine of the usual to two or one of the less usual.

Remembering that such harmonic sentences, like those of a typical text, are very much condensed, suggest that students see how long they can maintain a single harmony by means of interesting rhythms plus

Assignments and Special Projects

interesting melodies, with varying changes of register and dynamics. When the procedure is extended to more than a single harmony, suggest that students select the two or three harmonies to be used not only from the principal chords of the index but also from those less frequently used.

After they are acquainted with the index of harmonies discussed in Chapter Ten, ask that students write a composition based upon the index of a single note: an instrumental prelude or a song with the note rhythmically varied but maintained as a monotone by the singer. Then suggest that the note whose index is used be changed two or three times during the composition to admit the use of other indices, with a return to the original index for the last section of the composition.

Students may be encouraged to add other variations to the famous set based on "Chopsticks" written by the "Russian Five" (found in the second volume of the complete piano works of Liadov). They may be able to bring the set more nearly down to the present in vocabulary and style. Or, they might originate another set of variations exploiting the plurisignificance of the notes of another one-finger-melody, this time on the black keys of the keyboard — for instance, the setting of the well known Mother Goose rhyme "Peter, Peter, Pumpkin-eater."

Teaching Music Theory

When they are studying the harmonic clichés of the nineteenth century it would probably not ruin students' taste to ask them to write a rather sentimental and romantic song in which each one of these famous chromatic effects is used. Perhaps you should remind them that, when famous composers used these clichés, they did not sound hackneyed.

Students so often make unreasonable demands in vocal and instrumental range, or in matters of technique. We should ask them to meet their own demands by performance, or to find someone who will meet them. Then, it is a good idea to ask them to write some pieces for elementary piano students, not exceeding the limitations of grades I to III: few if any octaves, no unusual time-signatures, no key signatures beyond three sharps or flats, no chords with a stretch beyond a sixth, and no cross rhythms or mixed meters. Can they be original within the limitations fixed by the publishers of such materials? After they have worked within these narrow limitations, suggest that they create their own scales and use them for short compositions, keeping in mind the possibility of performance. Of course, all that the class writes should be performed if possible within the class, and, whenever feasible, outside the classroom in informal recitals or performances and rehearsals of student organizations.

[282]

Assignments and Special Projects

Assignments for keyboard harmony offer a great variety of practical drills, limited only by the ingenuity of the teacher. They can be combined with melodic improvisation if the harmonic sequence can be handled by the left hand; for instance, a waltz-pattern based upon the attendant diminished sevenths around each triad of a tonality.

A modulation from tonic to dominant with the formula: the old tonic, the dominant seventh or its inversion of the new key, a regular resolution to the new tonic, a pre-cadence chord of the student's choice, either diatonic or chromatic, and then a full cadence of I_4^6-V^7-I may be continued by transposition around the entire musical world or circle of fifths, returning to the point of origin. The student may be asked to report the time it takes him to make the round trip.

Playing dominant sevenths in root position with the complete chord in the right hand and an added root in the left hand (five voices), and following them by their respective tonics, in a succession of tonalities a half-step apart (C, B, B♭, etc.), reviews the spelling of these chords in all keys. Follow this sequence with a similar one having the tonalities a whole step apart. Then make each chord a dominant seventh and you have one of the famous chromatic generalizations, a chain of dominants.

The more uses you can find for any keyboard

[283]

drill, the better. As an illustration let us take the well known sequence of diatonic sevenths in the first conjugation: V^7-I^7-IV^7-$vii^{\circ 7}$-iii^7, etc. It is easier for students to play these in all tonalities when they are permitted to begin with five voices so that the complete spelling is available in the right hand. If we start with the root of the dominant seventh in the thumb of the right hand, after students have some facility in five parts ask them to drop the right thumb off the keyboard; and we now have four voices with the usual alternation of complete and incomplete sevenths. Playing the right hand alone with four parts introduces inversions, still in the first conjugation. Changing one voice (one finger) at a time, downward, introduces students to seventh chords in the second conjugation.

The keyboard can be used to demonstrate with one hand that any two dominant sevenths may be used in succession: ask the student to use common sense, holding over notes that remain the same, permitting a voice to change its own mind by an accidental (thus avoiding cross-relation), and moving to the nearest locations. This results in effective treatment and modulation to all tonalities, the second dominant seventh being in an inversion. Many other suggestions which may be carried out at the keyboard have been given in earlier chapters. How long will it take your students to play the usual augmented sixth effects inside, successively, the octaves C, B, B-♭, and so on until they reach C again? How long will it take them to play the following series of four chords V^9-iii^6-V^7-I, omitting the fifth of V^9 and playing thirds in the two upper voices, continuing around the complete circle of tonalities? The final third in C major becomes the top third of the dominant ninth in G major, and so on.

Another good idea is to ask the student to demonstrate that each chord of his harmonic index is really in the tonalities where he states that it is diatonic, starting with the chord in question and ending with a full cadence in each tonality. Assignments for the keyboard which result in much more radical treatment can be given; for instance, students may be asked to play a whole-tone scale, either as single notes or as augmented triads, in the left hand while playing in contrary motion in the right hand any of the following (first, a whole step apart and then a half-step apart): all major triads, all minor triads, alternate major and minor triads, all augmented triads, or any one of the five main species of seventh chords.

This chapter has not presented assignments in any systematic order, and those given are only a few of those which might be tried. They are intended merely to be suggestive of what can be done to vary the routine of the usual textbook. The teacher must first be sure that the fundamentals of conventional grammar are understood before unconventional assignments are given. This book must not be considered in any sense a substitute for the systematic presentation found in books on harmony. It has been written with the hope of sharing with other students and teachers some of the ideas which I have found interesting and useful.

Acknowledgments

THE AUTHOR gratefully acknowledges the permissions which have been granted for the use of copyrighted material. In addition to the publishers named when their illustrations appear, appreciation is expressed:

to Norma Millay Ellis for the quotation from Edna St. Vincent Millay's sonnet.

to *Harper's Magazine* for the quotations from *American Poetry's Golden Age* by Stanley Kunitz.

to James F. Hudson, editor, for permission to quote from the *Phi Gamma Delta Songbook*.

to W. W. Norton and Company for the quotations from Walter Piston's *Harmony*.

to M. Witmark and Sons for quotations from *Fundamentals of Musicianship* by Melville Smith and Max T. Krone. Book I, copyright, 1934, and Book II, copyright, 1937.

to Associated Music Publishers for permission to quote from Schönberg's *Sechs Kleine Klavierstücke*, Op. 19. (Copyright owner, Universal Edition, A. G., Vienna)

to Edwin F. Kalmus for the quotation from Bartok's *Bagatellen*.

to E. C. Schirmer Music Company for the quotation from Randall Thompson's *Alleluia*.

to *Harper's Magazine* for the quotations from *American* inson's *Aural Harmony* and John Alden Carpenter's *Krazey Kat* ballet.

Bibliography

ALBRECHTSBERGER, JOHANN GEORG. *Methods of Harmony, Figured Bass and Composition,* edited by Arnold Merrick, London: R. Cock, [1834].

ALCHIN, CAROLYN A. *Applied Harmony.* Los Angeles: c. by author, 1917.

ANDERSEN, ARTHUR OLAF. *Lessons in Harmony.* Boston: C. C. Birchard, 1938.

ANDREWS, HILDA. *Modern Harmony.* London: Oxford University Press, 1934.

ANGER, JOSEPH HUMFREY. *A Treatise on Harmony.* 3 vols. Boston: Boston Music Co., c. 1906-1912.

APEL, WILLI. *Die Fugue.* Berlin: Pflege Deutschkunst Verlag, 1932.

APPENZELLER, E. *Harmonielehre.* Zurich: Atlantis, 1947.

ATKISSON, HAROLD F. *Basic Counterpoint.* New York: McGraw, 1956.

BAIRSTOW, EDWARD C. *Counterpoint and Harmony.* London: Macmillan, 1945.

BALDWIN, RALPH LYMAN. *Harmony Simplified.* New York: M. Witmark, [c. 1933].

BARNES, A. F. *Practice in Modern Harmony.* London: Oxford University Press, 1937.

BERLIOZ, HECTOR. *Treatise on Orchestration,* revised by R. Strauss and transl. by Theodore Front. New York: E. F. Kalmus, 1948.

BIGELOW, EARL H. *et al. Creative-Analytical Theory of Music.* 2 vols. Chicago: FitzSimons, 1948.

Bibliography

BLOCH, WALDEMER. *Neue Harmonielehre für Schulgebrauch.* Graz: Leykan, 1948.

BRAHMS, JOHANNES. *Oktaven und Quinten,* edited by H. Schenker. Wien: Universal Edition, [c. 1933].

BRAUNER, RUDOLPH F. *Vom Dreiklang zum Zwölftonakkord.* Wien: Verlag für Jugend und Volk, 1949.

BUCK, PERCY C. *Unfigured Harmony.* Oxford: Clarendon Press, 1911.

CARNER, MOSCO. *A Study of Twentieth Century Harmony.* London: J. Williams, [1942].

CHADWICK, GEORGE W. *Harmony.* Boston: B. F. Wood, c. 1925.

CHAILLEY, JACQUES. *Traité historique d'analyse musicale.* Paris: Leduc, 1951.

CHERUBINI, LUIGI. *A Treatise on Counterpoint and Fugue,* transl. by Mary C. Clarke, revised by Joseph Bennett. London: Novello, 1884.

COERNE, LOUIS ADOLPHE. *The Evolution of Modern Orchestration.* New York: Macmillan, 1908.

CONUS, GEORG EDUARD. *A Critical Study of Traditional Theory in the Field of Musical Form* (in Russian). Moscow: Gossudarstvennoe Muzikalnoe Izdatelstvo, 1932.

CORDER, FREDERICK. *Modern Musical Composition.* London: Curwen, [n.d.].

CRIST, BAINBRIDGE. *The Art of Setting Words to Music.* New York: C. Fischer, 1944.

CUTTER, BENJAMIN. *Harmonic Analysis.* Boston: O. Ditson, [1902].

DAVISON, ARCHIBALD T. *The Technique of Choral Composition.* Cambridge, Mass.: Harvard University Press, 1945.

DAY, ALFRED. *A Treatise on Harmony.* London: Kramer & Beale, 1845.

[289]

Bibliography

DEMUTH, NORMAN. *A Course in Musical Composition*. London: Bosworth, 1951.

DICKENMANN, PAUL. *Die Entwicklung der Harmonik bei A. Skrjabin*. Bern: Paul Haupt, 1935.

DILLER, ANGELA. *First Theory Book*. New York: G. Schirmer, [c. 1921].

—————. *Keyboard Music Study* (Books 1-2). New York: G. Schirmer, [c. 1936].

DUBOIS, THEODORE. *Traité de Countrepoint et du Fugue*. Paris: Heugel, 1901.

EGERT, PAUL. *Die Klaviersonate im Zeitalter der Romantik*. Leipzig: published by the author, 1934.

ERPF, HERMANN. *Studien zur Harmonie und Klangtechnik*. Leipzig: Breitkopf u. Härtel, 1927.

FEDERHOFER, HELMUT. *Beiträge zur musikalischen Gestaltanalyse*. Wien: Akademische Druck u. Verlags-gesellschaft, 1950.

FINNEY, ROSS LEE. *The Game of Harmony*. New York: Harcourt, Brace and Co., 1947.

FOOTE, ARTHUR AND SPALDING, WALTER R. *Modern Harmony*. Boston: A. P. Schmidt, [c. 1905].

FORNEBERG, ERICH. *Der Geist der neuen Musik*. Kassel-Wilhelmshöhe: Bärenreiter, 1957.

FORSYTH, CECIL. *Orchestration*. New York: Macmillan, 1942.

FORTE, ALLEN. *Tonal Harmony in Concept and Practice*. New York: Holt, Rinehart and Winston, 1962.

FUX, JOHANN JOSEPH. *Steps to Parnassus,* transl. and edited by Alfred Mann and John St. Edmunds. New York: Norton, 1945.

GANNETT, KENT (compiler). *Bach's Harmonic Progressions*. Philadelphia: O. Ditson, [1942].

GEDALGE, ANDRE. *Traité de la Fugue*. Paris: Enoch, 1890.

Bibliography

GILSON, PAUL. *Quintes, Octaves, Secondes et Polytone.* Bruxelles: Schott Frères, 1922.

GOETSCHIUS, PERCY. *Applied Counterpoint,* Fifth edition. New York: G. Schirmer, 1915.

——————. *Exercises in Elementary Counterpoint.* New York: G. Schirmer, 1910.

GRABNER, HERMANN. *Regers Harmonik.* München: Halbreiter, 1920.

——————. *Die Funktionstheorie Hugo Riemann.* München: Halbreiter, 1923.

GULDENSTEIN, GUSTAV. *Die Gegenwertigkeit in der Musik.* Zurich: Hug, 1933.

GUNTHER, SIEGFRIED. *Moderne Polyphonie.* Berlin: Gruyter, 1930.

HABA, ALOIS. *Neue Harmonielehre.* Leipzig: F. Kistner u. C. F. Siegel, 1927.

HAMBURGER, P. *Subdominante und Wechseldominant.* Wiesbaden: Breitkopf u. Härtel, 1956.

HANSON, HOWARD. *Harmonic Materials of Modern Music.* New York: Appleton-Century-Crofts, 1960.

HAUER, JOSEPH M. *Zwölftontechnik, die Lehre von den Tropen.* Wien: Universal Edition, 1926.

HEACOX, ARTHUR E. *A Guide through the Lessons in Harmony by Heacox and Lehmann.* Oberlin, O.: A. G. Comings, 1912.

——————. *Harmony for Ear, Eye and Keyboard.* Philadelphia: O. Ditson, [c. 1922].

——————. *Project Lessons in Orchestration.* Boston: O. Ditson, 1928.

HEUERMANN-HAMILTON, ANNA. *Keyboard Harmony and Transposition.* Chicago: Clayton Summy, 1916.

HILL, ALFRED. *Melody and Harmony.* Boston: A. P. Schmidt, [n.d.].

Bibliography

HINDEMITH, PAUL. *The Craft of Musical Composition*, Books I and II, transl. by Arthur Mendel. New York: Associated Music Publishers. Mainz: B. Schotts Söhne, 1937.

——————. *Elementary Training for Musicians*. New York: Associated Music Publishers, [c. 1946].

——————. *A Concentrated Course in Traditional Harmony*. New York: Associated Music Publishers, Book I, c. 1944, Book II, [c. 1953].

——————. *Einleitende Bemerkungen zur neuer Fassung, Das Marienleben*. Mainz: Schott, 1948.

HULL, ARTHUR EAGLEFIELD. *Modern Harmony*. London: Augener, [1915].

HUTCHINGS, ARTHUR. *The Invention and Composition of Music*. London: Novello, 1958.

D'INDY, VINCENT. *Cours de composition musicale*. Paris: A. Durand, 1912.

JACOB, GORDON. *Orchestral Technique*. London: Oxford University Press, 1931.

JADASSOHN, SALOMON. *A Course of Instruction in Canon and Fugue,* transl. by Gusav Wolff. Leipzig: Breitkopf u. Härtel, 1929.

JAKOBIK, ALBERT. *Die assoziative Harmonik in den Klavierwerken Claude Debussys*. Würzburg: Tribsch, 1940.

JAQUES-DALCROZE, EMILE. *The Jaques-Dalcroze Method of Eurhythmics*. London: Novello, 1920.

——————. *Rhythm, Music and Education,* transl. by Harold F. Rubinstein. New York: Putnam, 1921.

JEPPESEN, KNUD. *The Style of Palestrina and the Dissonance,* transl. by Margaret W. Hamerik. Oxford: H. Milford, 1927.

——————. *Counterpoint,* transl. by Glen Haydon. New York: Prentice-Hall, 1939.

Bibliography

KARG-ELERT, SIGFRID. *Polaristische Klang- und Tonalitätslehre.* Leipzig: Leuckart, 1932.

KAYSER, HANS. *Lehrbuch der Harmonik.* Zurich: Occident Verlag, 1950.

KENNAN, KENT. *Orchestration.* New York: Prentice-Hall, 1952.

——————. *Counterpoint.* New York: Prentice-Hall, 1959.

KIEKERT, INGEBORG. *Die musikalische Form in den Werken Carl Orff's.* Regensburg: Gustav Bosse, 1957.

KIRSCH, ERNST. *Wesen und Aufbau der Lehre von den harmonischen Funktionen.* Leipzig: Breitkopf u. Härtel, 1928.

KITSON, C. H. *The Art of Counterpoint.* London: Oxford University Press, 1907.

——————. *Invertible Counterpoint and Canon.* London: Oxford University Press, 1927.

——————. *Studies in Fugue.* London: Oxford University Press, 1928.

——————. *The Elements of Fugal Construction.* London: Oxford University Press, 1929.

——————. *Applied Strict Counterpoint.* Oxford: Clarendon Press, 1931.

——————. *Counterpoint for Beginners.* London: Oxford University Press, 1937.

KLOTZ, HANS. *Neue Harmoniewissenschaft.* Leipzig: Robert Noske, 1927.

KOECHLIN, CHARLES. *Traité d'harmonie.* 3 vols. Paris: M. Eschig, 1927-1930.

KOHS, ELLIS B. *Music Theory.* 2 vols. New York: Oxford University Press, 1960 and 1961.

KOLINSKI, M. *Konsonanz als Grundlage einer neuer Akkordlehre.* Brünn: Rohrer, 1937.

KRENEK, ERNST. *Studies in Counterpoint.* New York: G. Schirmer, [c. 1940].

Bibliography

KROHN, ILMARI. *Erneuerung des musikalischen Unterrichts.* Den Haag: Bulletin de la Union musicologique, III-1, 1923.

—————. *Anton Bruckners Symphonien: Untersuchung über Formenbau und Stimmungsgehalt.* Helsinki: Suomalainen Tiedeak Taemian Toimituksia, 1955-56.

KURTH, ERNST. *Die Voraussetzungen der theoretischen Harmonik.* Bern: Max Drechsel, 1913.

—————. *Grundlagen des linearen Kontrapunkt.* Bern: Krompholz, 1917.

—————. *Romantische Harmonik und ihre Krise in Wagners Tristan.* Berlin: M. Hesse, 1923.

LEHMANN, F. J. *Harmonic Analysis.* Oberlin, O.: A. G. Comings, 1910.

LEICHTENTRITT, HUGO. *Musical Form.* Cambridge, Mass.: Harvard University Press, 1951.

LEVARIE, SIGMUND. *Fugue and Form.* Chicago: copyright by the author, 1941.

—————. *Fundamentals of Harmony.* New York: Ronald Press, [1954].

LORENZ, ALFRED. *Das Geheimnis der Form bei R. Wagner.* Berlin: Max Hesse, 4 vols., 1924, 1926, 1931, 1933.

LOUIS, RUDOF AND THUILLE, LUDWIG. *Harmonielehre,* eighth edition. Stuttgart: Klett, 1913.

LYTLE, VICTOR VAUGHN. *The Theory and Practice of Strict Counterpoint.* Philadelphia: O. Ditson, 1940.

MCCONATHY, OSBOURNE, *et al. An Approach to Harmony.* New York: Silver Burdett, [c. 1927].

MCHOSE, ALLEN IRVINE. *The Contrapuntal Harmonic Technique of the 18th Century.* New York: F. S. Crofts, 1947.

—————. *Basic Principles of the Technique of 18th and 19th*

Bibliography

Century Composition. New York: Appleton-Century-Crofts, [1951].

McHose, Allen I. and Tibbs, Ruth Northrup. *Sight-singing Manual*. New York: Appleton-Century-Crofts, [1944].

McKay, George Frederick. *The Technique of Modern Harmony*. Seattle, Wash.: copyright by the author, 1941.

Macpherson, Stewart. *Practical Counterpoint*. London: J. Williams, 1907.

——————. *Form in Music*. London: J. Williams, 1915.

——————. *Melody and Harmony*. London: J. Williams, [c. 1920].

——————. *Studies in the Art of Counterpoint*. London: J. Williams, 1927.

Merritt, Arthur Tillman. *Sixteenth-Century Polyphony*. Cambridge, Mass.: Harvard University Press, 1939.

Mersmann, Hans. *Angewandte Musikästhetik*. Berlin: Max Hesse, 1926.

Messiaen, Olivier. *Technique de mon langage musical,* transl. by John Satterfield. 2 vols. Paris: A. Leduc, 1944, [transl. c. 1956].

Miller, Horace A. *New Harmonic Devices*. Chicago: Lyon and Healy, 1930.

——————. *Modal Trends in Modern Music*. Altadena: Cornell, 1941.

Minotti, Giovanni. *Die Geheimdokumente der Davidsbündler*. Leipzig: Seeingräber Verlag, [c. 1934].

Mitchell, William J. *Elementary Harmony*. New York: Prentice-Hall, 1939.

Morris, R. O. *Foundations of Practical Harmony and Counterpoint*. London: Macmillan, 1936.

——————. *Introduction to Counterpoint*. London: Oxford University Press, 1948.

[295]

Bibliography

MULLER VON KULM, WALTER. *Grundriss der Harmonielehre.* Basel: Amerbach, 1948.

MURPHY, HOWARD A. AND STRINGHAM, EDWIN J. *Creative Harmony and Musicianship.* New York: Prentice-Hall, 1951.

Kegan Paul, Trench and Trubner, 1925.

NERN, ALLAN. *Simplified sight-singing.* Philadelphia: Elkan-Vogel, [c. 1940].

NEWTON, ERNEST RICHARD. *How to Compose a Song.* London:

NORDEN, HUGO. *Harmony and Its Application in Violin Playing.* Boston: E. C. Schirmer, 1937.

OLDROYD, GEORGE. *The Technique and Spirit of Fugue.* London: Oxford University Press, 1948.

————. *Polyphonic Writing for Voices in Six or Eight Parts.* London: Oxford University Press, 1953.

OREM, PRESTON WARE. *Manual of Fugue.* Bryn Mawr: Presser, 1939.

PEARCE, CHARLES W. *Students' Counterpoint.* New York: G. Schirmer, 1926.

PERSICHETTI, VINCENT. *Twentieth-Century Harmony.* New York: Norton, 1961.

PISTON, WALTER. *Principles of Harmonic Analysis.* Boston: E. C. Schirmer, 1933.

————. *Harmony.* New York: Norton, 1941.

————. *Counterpoint.* New York: Norton, 1947.

————. *Orchestration.* New York: Norton, 1955.

PORTER, QUINCY. *A Study of Fugue Writing.* Boston: Loomis, 1951.

PROCTER, LELAND H. *Tonal Counterpoint.* Dubuque, Iowa: Brown, 1957.

PROUT, EBENEZER. *Fugue.* London: Augener, 1891.

Bibliography

——————. *Double Counterpoint and Canon.* London: Augener, 1891.

——————. *Fugal Analysis,* London: Augener, 1892.

——————. *Musical Form.* London: Augener, [1893].

——————. *Applied Form.* London: Augener, [1895].

——————. *Counterpoint.* London: Augener, [n.d.].

——————. *Harmony.* London: Augener (16th edition), [c. 1903].

PROUT, LOUIS B. *Sidelights on Harmony.* London: Augener, 1902].

RATNER, LEONARD G. *Harmony: Structure and Style.* New York: McGraw-Hill, 1962.

READ, GARDNER. *Thesaurus of Orchestral Devices.* New York: Pitman, [1953].

REGER, MAX. *Beiträge zur Modulationslehre.* Leipzig: C. F. Kahnt, 1904.

RICHARDSON, A. MADELEY. *Helps to Fugue Writing.* New York: H. W. Gray, 1930.

——————. *Fundamental Counterpoint.* New York: American Book Co., 1936.

RIEMANN, HUGO. *Musikalische Syntaxis.* Leipzig: Breitkopf u. Härtel, 1877.

——————. *Handbuch der Harmonielehre.* 2d ed. Leipzig: Breitkopf u. Härtel, 1887. *Harmony Simplified, or the Theory of Tonal Functions,* (transl.). London: Augener, [n.d.].

——————. *Grundriss der Kompositionslehre.* Berlin: Hesse, 1916.

RIMSKY-KORSAKOFF, NICHOLAS. *Principles of Orchestration.* Berlin: Edition Russe de Musique, 1923. A reprint, transl. by Edward Agate, New York: E. F. Kalmus.

Bibliography

——————. *Practical Manual of Harmony,* transl. by Joseph Achron. New York: C. Fischer, 1930.

ROBINSON, FRANKLIN W. *Aural Harmony.* New York: G. Schirmer, 1918. (The revision published by Hill-Coleman, 1936, is quite different.)

ROCHBERG, GEORGE. *The Hexachord and its Relation to the 12-tone row.* Bryn Mawr: Presser, 1955.

RÖTTGER, HEINZ. *Die Formproblem bei Richard Strauss.* Berlin: Junker u. Dünnhaupt, 1937.

ROGERS, BERNARD. *The Art of Orchestration.* New York: Appleton-Century-Crofts, [1951].

RUFER, JOSEPH. *Die Komposition mit zwölf Tönen.* Berlin: Max Hesse, 1952. (English translation by Humphrey Searle. New York: Macmillan, 1954.)

SALZER, FELIX. *Structural Hearing.* New York: Charles Boni, 1952.

SCHENKER, HEINRICH. *Neue musikalische Theorien und Phantasien.* Cotta, 1906: Vol. I, *Harmony,* edited by Oswald Jonas, transl. by Elizabeth Mann Borgese. Chicago: University of Chicago Press, 1954.

——————. Bd. II/1, *Kontrapunkt.* Wien: Universal Edition, 1908.

——————. Bd. II/2, *Kontrapunkt.* Wien: Universal Edition, 1922.

——————. Bd. III, *Der Freie Satz.* Wien: Universal Edition, 1935.

——————. *Erläuterungs Ausgaben der letzen fünf Sonaten Beethovens.* Wien: Universal Edition, Op. 109 (1913), Op. 110 (1914), Op. 111 (1915), Op. 101 (1920-21); the autograph for Op. 106 was lost.

SCHILLINGER, JOSEPH. *Kaleidophone.* New York: M. Witmark, 1940.

Bibliography

——————. *The Schillinger System of Musical Composition.* 2 vols. New York: C. Fischer, [1946].

SCHLIEDER, FREDERICK W. *Lyric Composition through Improvisation.* Boston: C. C. Birchard, 1927.

SCHÖNBERG, ARNOLD. *Harmonielehre.* Wien: Universal Edition, [c. 1922].

——————. transl. in part under title *Theory of Harmony* by Robert D. W. Adams. New York: Philosophical Library, [1948].

——————. *Models for Beginners in Composition.* New York: G. Schirmer, 1943.

——————. *Style and Idea.* New York: Philosophical Library, [c. 1950].

——————. *Structural Functions of Harmony.* New York: Norton, [1954].

SCHWARTZ, G. F. *Harmonic Analysis.* Boston: Badger, 1917.

SEARLE, HUMPHREY. *Twentieth Century Counterpoint.* New York: J. de Graff, 1954.

SMITH, MELVILLE AND KRONE, MAX. *Fundamentals of Musicianship.* 2 vols. New York: M. Witmark, [c. 1934-1937].

SMITS VAN WAESBERGHE, JOSEPH. *A Textbook of Melody.* Nijmegen, Netherlands: American Institute of Musicology, 1955.

SODERLUND, GUSTAVE FREDERIC. *Direct Approach to Counterpoint in 16th Century Style.* New York: Appleton-Century-Crofts, 1947.

STAINER, JOHN. *Composition.* London: Novello, 1880.

STANFORD, CHARLES V. *Musical Composition.* London: Macmillan, 1911.

TOCH, ERNST. *The Shaping Forces in Music.* New York: Criterion, [c. 1948].

Bibliography

TROTTER, T. H. YORKE. *The Making of Musicians; the Rhythmic Method of Music Teaching.* London: H. Jenkins, 1914.

TSCHAIKOWSKI, PETER. *Leitfaden zum praktischen Erlernen der Harmonie,* transl. by Paul Juon. Leipzig: Jurgenson, 1900.

TWEEDY, DONALD NICHOLS. *Manual of Harmonic Technique Based on the Practice of J. S. Bach.* Boston: O. Ditson, [c. 1928].

VERNEVIL, CHALUEZ DE. *Genuphonic Grammar.* London: Brown, Green and Longman, 1850.

VILLERMAIN, LOUIS. *Traité d'harmonie ultramoderne.* Paris: published by the author, 1911.

VINCENT, JOHN N. *The Diatonic Modes in Modern Music.* Berkeley: University of California Press, 1951.

WAGNER, JOSEPH FREDERICK. *Orchestration.* New York: McGraw-Hill, 1959.

WARBURTON, ANNIE O. *Harmony for Schools and Colleges.* London: Longmans, Green and Co., 1938.

WARTISCH, OTTO. *Studien zur Harmonik des musikalischen Impressionismus.* Kaiserlautern: Rohr, 1930.

WEDGE, GEORGE ANSON. *Keyboard Harmony.* New York: G. Schirmer, [c. 1924].

————. *Applied Harmony.* New York: G. Schirmer, [c. 1930].

WEIDIG, ADOLF. *Harmonic Material and Its Uses.* Chicago: Clayton F. Summy, 1923.

WIDOR, CH.-MARIE. *The Technique of the Modern Orchestra,* transl. by Edward Suddard. London: Joseph Williams, 1906.

WOLPERT, F. A. *Neue Harmonik.* Regensburg: Bosse Verlag, 1953.

Bibliography

ZIEHN, BERNARD. *Harmonie und Modulationslehre.* Berlin
(Grosslichtenfeld): Sulzer, 1887.

——————. *Five and Six-part Harmonies and How to Use
Them.* Milwaukee, Wisc.: Wm. A. Kaun, 1911.

——————. *Manual of Harmony.* Milwaukee, Wisc.: Wm. A.
Kaun, n.d. and Leipzig: C. F. Fleischer, [c. 1907].